Cardinal Principles of Governance

Cardinal Principles of Governance

✦

Strengthening The Governance Of Nonprofit Organizations In America's Communities

A Step-by-Step Guide to Responsible Nonprofit Governance Full of Innovative Ideas and Resources

Arnold Clickstein

iUniverse, Inc.
New York Lincoln Shanghai

Cardinal Principles of Governance
Strengthening The Governance Of Nonprofit Organizations In America's Communities

iUniverse books may be ordered through booksellers or by contacting:

iUniverse
2021 Pine Lake Road, Suite 100
Lincoln, NE 68512
www.iuniverse.com
1-800-Authors (1-800-288-4677)

ISBN: 978-0-595-41714-8 (pbk)
ISBN: 978-0-595-86055-5 (ebk)

Printed in the United States of America

If men were angels, there would be no need for government.

—James Madison

Contents

Acknowledgments

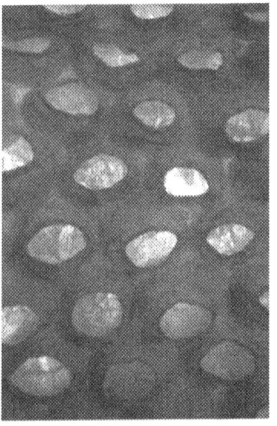

Reprinted with permission of Lara Lepionka

Winchester, Massachusetts
December 2006

This book is dedicated to my wonderful wife, Sue, and our children and grandchildren, whose love buoyed me through each revision. I am especially grateful to Sue and our youngest son, Noah, for their encouragement, support, and patience with me when I hovered too long at the computer, worked on weekends, or gave an all-too-short "good night." I also am deeply appreciative of Sue who proofread each draft, asked good questions, and made excellent suggestions.

I also offer my heartfelt thanks to Michael Kaiser and Gilbert Osborn who critiqued the fourth manuscript. Michael read and praised my original paper on governance, which stimulated me to write this book. He also assisted me with research on nonprofit statistics, Alexis de Tocqueville, and corporate governance. He provided me with valuable input, including urging me to expand the Red Cross case. Gil also read and critiqued the fourth draft, providing me with wise and valued input.

The subtitle of this book was eventually generated from the action of Joel Nitzberg, Director of the Institute for Lifelong Learning and Community Building at Cambridge College, Cambridge, Massachusetts. He invited me to lead a seminar on *Improving the Governance of Nonprofits in Our Communities*. I thank him for that wonderful experience.

Finally, I also am very grateful to Lara Lepionka, an energetic, bright, and talented Gloucester artist, who contributed her artwork and helped me with the graphics in the introduction.

—Arnold Clickstein

Introduction

Time present and time past
Are both perhaps presenting time future
A time future contained in time past.
—T. S. Eliot

I spent thirty-plus years in nonprofit organizations teaching, leading, and most importantly, learning. I watched the nonprofit sector grow while certain institutions and organizations floundered, misused the public trust given to them, or did business as if they were a "mom and pop" grocery store. I learned from Stephen Covey that if an individual wants to really master what he has learned, then as soon as possible he has to go out and teach it. Thus this book is an effort to teach what I learned about the role of governance in nonprofit organizations, a crucial aspect of the nonprofit world.

The nonprofit industry in the United States is enormous. For those of us connected to it in some way, either as a donor, staff member, board member, member, client, or plain tax-paying citizen, we need to understand that governance represents the building blocks of nonprofit organizations. This book represents an opportunity to gain some perspective on nonprofits and the important role of governance in them. Even more important, this book outlines the tasks that governing boards need to attend to if their organizations are to meet the challenges of the twenty-first century. Finally, the book provides an opportunity to think and rethink about how nonprofits are governed.

Today more than at any other time during the last twenty-five years, nonprofit organizations in the United States are under the scrutiny of state governments, the federal government, think tanks, "watch dog" organizations, and concerned individuals. A recent report by the Brookings Institution indicates that financial management is overlooked often enough to cause public confidence in charitable organizations to stagnate, and the current situation shows "no signs of recovering. Scandals ... have continued to alter what people think of charities."[1] Charities are facing intense scrutiny, which is leading "to demands for greater financial accountability and tougher regulations," while the general public loses confidence in the nonprofit sector.[2]

At the same time, the nonprofit sector continues to grow in America. Our federal and state governments have invested power in the governing boards of these organizations that are an integral part of American life. By definition, a *governing board* is "an organized group of people with the collective authority to control and foster an institution that is usually administrated by a qualified executive and staff."[3] To understand the problem of why nonprofits are under the scrutiny of the government and the public, we must explore it at its roots, for nonprofits are everywhere.

While nonprofit organizations have missions, this does not ensure that they are well run or that they will overcome the fissures that may be plaguing them. To meet the challenges organizations face in this new century, boards and their CEOs need to adopt a broader perspective with respect to their responsibilities. For some, their roles are overly simplified, overlooked, or stepped into without knowledge and experience. They are completely unprepared to fill them.

Perhaps we have never understood the parameters, limitations, and value bases that operate in the organizations with which we are associated. Whatever the reason, it is important we understand the platform from which we need to start operating, for we really need to begin thinking about creating a new vision for ourselves and our organizations.

In global terms, there are four key perspectives that CEOs and members of governing boards need to adopt if they are to successfully support, guide, and lead our organizations in the next quarter of a century:

- First, it is important to gain an *organizational sense of place*, which is both geographical and historical. This includes obtaining a perspective on the history of the organizations, seeing how they fit into the communities they serve and the nonprofit scene in America, as well as understanding the historical perspective of how the nonprofit world we observe today evolved from the early American colonies.

- Second, we need to fully comprehend our *fiduciary role* within nonprofit organizations, not only in terms of the tasks before us, but of the full range of responsibilities this role entails.

- Third, we need to explore and buy into the importance of *strategic planning* and thinking.

- Finally, instead of consuming valuable time listening to committee reports, all of us need to spend more of it identifying the important issues, discussing them, reflecting on our discussions, and working toward consensus either to resolve the issues or create a plan to deal with them. I call this process the *issue engagement task*.

These four keys are ensconced within a ring of ethics, morals, and values I call the *ring of ethical engagement*, which requires us to be ethically and morally engaged.

In addition to this concept, we will briefly explore the role of *assessment* in our nonprofit world and how to apply Peter Senge's concepts of *learning environment* and *shared visions*, along with some of my observations, to the management of nonprofit organizations.

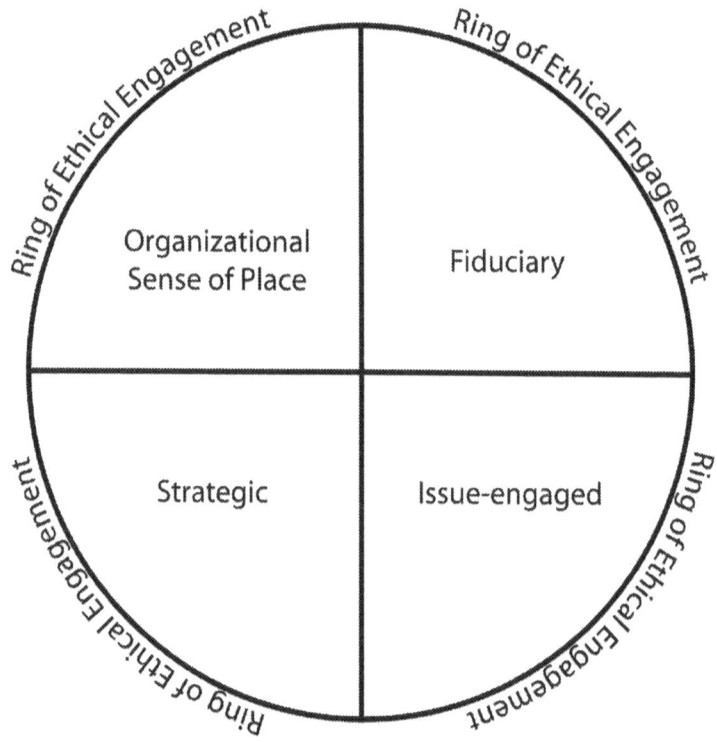

Let's examine our nonprofits in the context of the nonprofit world today. We begin by gaining our organizational sense of place. It is here we can gather a more global view of the nonprofit world. It's not that we want to return to earlier days, but rather to achieve a more worldly perspective. By understanding the past, we gain a perspective on how the organizations we are concerned about got to where they are today. It is here that we can ground ourselves in an organization's foundation and geography so that we can better see our way forward and contribute to its future.

Let's begin our exploration.

1

The Evolution of Nonprofit Organizations in America

Americans of all ages, all conditions, and
all dispositions, constantly form associations …
From that moment, they are a power seen from
afar, whose actions serve for an example.
—Alexis de Tocqueville

The nonprofit sector in the United States is quite large. Governing boards have a crucial part to play in their evolution and governance, especially given the size of this sector, as any particular organization is just one of approximately 1.4 million nonprofit organizations in the United States. Consider this as well: approximately thirty thousand new nonprofits are created every year.[1]

Here in Massachusetts where I live, there are 35,133 nonprofit organizations. Between 1996 and 2004, the Commonwealth had a 59.9 percent increase in the number of 501(c)(3) public charities and an 11.6 percent increase in the number of private foundations. Cultural organizations in the state provide forty thousand jobs alone. The total economic impact on the state for this segment amounts to $4.2 billion. Nationally, the arts segment generates $134 billion in economic activity every year, including $24.4 billion in federal, state, and local taxes.[2]

The number of Americans employed in the nonprofit sector has more than doubled in the last twenty-five years and today approaches some 12.5 million workers, or 9.5 percent of the total workforce. Approximately 5.7 million people also do volunteer work in our nonprofit organizations.[3]

Most nonprofit employees work in the healthcare (42 percent) and education (22 percent) fields. The number of people employed in the nonprofit sector probably will reach fifteen million by 2010, with significant growth in the areas of health and human/social services.[4]

Other economic indicators from the nonprofit sector include a Giving USA 2004 report that charitable giving in the United States. increased at the fastest rate in the three consecutive years ending in 2003, rising some 2.8 percent to $240.7 billion. Similarly, the U.S. Department of Commerce indicates that nonprofit organizations in America spent $236.5 billion in 2003 while their revenue amounted to more than $254.5 billion.[5]

Besides charitable, educational, health, and social service organizations, an entire group of organizations has been given tax-exempt status in fields such as professional athletics and real estate, to name but two. They are listed in *Appendix A*. Resources for statistics about the nonprofit sector are available in *Appendix B*.

On a broader scale, the nonprofit sector is a massive economic as well as social force that is expanding rapidly throughout the world, partly in response to growing doubts about the ability of nation-states to respond to social welfare, developmental, and environmental problems or cultural needs. Many countries have adopted the U.S. nonprofit model to run their cultural, educational, health, and social service organizations.

Outside the United States, nonprofits are often referred to as nongovernmental organizations or NGOs. According to Johns Hopkins University's Center for Civil Society Studies, in the twenty-two countries it studied, nearly nineteen million people were employed in the nonprofit sector, making it a $1.1 trillion (U.S.) industry. If treated as a separate economy, it would be the eighth largest in the world.[6]

While it is easy to identify the financial impact the nonprofit sector has on the respective countries where it exists, the contribution this sector makes to individuals and communities within our states, our country, and the world is also enormous. Thus it is important to understand how this sector got to be so large.

The Roots of Governance in Nonprofit Organizations

Sören Kierkegaard wrote, "Life must be understood backward, but it must be lived forward."[7] Let's look backward for a moment and explore the roots of governance and nonprofit organizations in America. How did the nonprofit world in the United States evolve, and how did it get to be so large a sector of American life? The best place to begin is with a brief review of how governance evolved in the English-speaking world overall.

The word *governance* means government and the exercise of control or authority, as it refers to a system of government. The word is derived from the Middle Latin word *gubernantia*, which evolved into the Middle English word *governaunce*. Governing bodies generally function by rules of order and precedents commonly employed by deliberative assemblies. Such rules are intended to maintain decorum, ascertain the will of the majority, preserve the rights of the minority, and facilitate the orderly transaction of the business of an assembly. Thus governance functions on rules of order.

Rules of order originated in the early British parliaments. In the sixteenth century, Sir Thomas Smith wrote a formal statement of procedures for the House of Commons that was published in 1583 as *Lex Parliamentaria*. It served as a pocket manual for members of Parliament and was gradually expanded until it included many precedents that are now familiar:

1. Only one subject should be discussed at a time (1581).

2. The chair must always call for the negative vote (1604).

3. Personal attacks and indecorous behavior are to be avoided in debate (1604)."He that digresseth from the Matter to fall upon the Person ought to be suppressed by the Speaker … No reviling or nipping words must be used."

4. Debate must be limited to the merits of the question (1610). "A member speaking, and his speech, seeming impertinent, and there being much hissing and spitting, it was conceived as a rule that Mr. Speaker may stay impertinent speeches."[8]

These procedures, decisions, and precedents developed in the British parliament that came to be known as parliamentary law were brought to America by the colonists. Operating under written charters and grants, the colonists ran the colonies using this same parliamentary process in all of their meetings, be they legislative, town, or parish. This experience influenced the framing of the Constitution of the United States in 1787.[9]

Thomas Jefferson was the first to interpret and define parliamentary principles for the new American government. In 1801 while Jefferson was vice president and presiding officer of the Senate, he discovered, much to his dismay, that the Senate was not following any consistent set of rules, instead referring matters to the president to decide. "Jefferson had approached his single vice-presidential duty of presiding over the Senate with feelings of inadequacy. John Adams, who had held the job since the Senate's founding in 1789,

knew a great deal about Senate procedure and of—equal importance—about British parliamentary operations. Yet, despite Adams'
knowledge, senators routinely criticized him for his arbitrary and
inconsistent parliamentary rulings."[10] Thus in 1801, Jefferson wrote
A Manual of Parliamentary Practice in which he created a set of rules
for the president and Senate to follow as well as "for himself and
future presiding officers."[11] Years later, the House of Representatives adopted Jefferson's *Manual* as a "partial guide to its own
proceedings."[12] *Robert's Rules of Order* indicates that "the authority
of the *Manual* became established through its adoption by state legislatures and by other groups."[13]

Several decades later, it became evident that with the formation
of various kinds of organizations (political, cultural, scientific, and
religious), a set of governing rules were needed that met the needs of
non-legislative bodies. In 1832, Luther Stearns Cushing became the
clerk of the Massachusetts House of Representatives, an office he
held for fourteen years. Among his prolific writings was a parliamentary manual with a title similar to Jefferson's, the *Manual of
Parliamentary Practice*, which eventually became known as "Cushing's Manual." He later wrote another treatise, *Elements of the Law
and Practice of Legislative Assemblies*.[14] This was the earliest attempt
by an American to create a manual of parliamentary practice that
could serve "assemblies of every description … especially … those
not legislative in their character."[15]

Later in the century, a U.S. Army officer, Brigadier General
Henry Martyn Robert, was stationed in New Bedford, Massachusetts recovering from a tropical fever he contracted while in Panama.
While there he was asked to preside over a meeting at his church,
but when he quickly lost control of the situation, he realized he
didn't know how to run a meeting. "Embarrassed, he sought guidance from existing manuals of parliamentary procedure and found

them to be useless, even occasionally absurd. Robert set out to be a student of parliamentary procedure."[16]

In 1867, Robert was promoted and sent to San Francisco, where he and his wife worked in a number of organizations with people from every part of the country seeking to improve social conditions in San Francisco.[17] Robert served on the boards of the YMCA and the First Baptist Church. At the YMCA meetings, disputes over procedural matters often arose, with the chair's authority frequently challenged. The First Baptist Church's "Constitution and Rules of Order" were filled with platitudes and inadequate guidelines for running meetings. "Convinced of the need for some sort of parliamentary authority," Robert soon began to write a "sixteen-page parliamentary guide for the societies that he and his wife had joined, but he soon decided that a generic guide for all organizations and associations was needed."[18]

In 1871, Robert was transferred to Portland, Oregon, where his contact with organizations "strengthened ideas which had begun to crystallize in San Francisco."[19] There was a need "to enable civic minded people to belong to several organizations or to move to new localities without constantly encountering different parliamentary rules. In 1874, Robert was transferred to Wisconsin. During a harsh, snowy winter, he completed and published in 1879 his *Pocket Manual of Rules of Order for Deliberative Assemblies*. A year later it was published as *Robert's Rules of Order*.[20] "From that time on, Robert solicited letters and comments and, in response, revised his manual, with the most complete and important revision published in 1915, eight years after his death."[21]

While an abridged version (176 pages) is available today, the authorized, unabridged edition comprises over 643 pages. The use of *Robert's Rules of Order* provides an underpinning of the governance process.

Robert was right on target in his observation that the various societies being created had a need for some parliamentary procedure. According to Alexis de Tocqueville, the French political scientist and historian, there were many committees or associations in America. In the 1800s, he wrote a four-volume analysis of the American political and social system based on his trips to America, entitled *Democracy in America*.

In it he observed, "Americans of all ages, all conditions, and all dispositions constantly form associations. They have not only commercial and manufacturing companies, in which all take part, but associations of a thousand other kinds, religious, moral, serious, futile, general or restricted, enormous or diminutive. The Americans make associations to give entertainments, to found seminaries, to build inns, to construct churches, to diffuse books, to send missionaries to the antipodes; in this manner they have found hospitals, prisons, and schools. If it is proposed to inculcate some truth or to foster some feeling by the encouragement of great example, they form a society. Wherever at the head of some new undertaking you see the government in France or a man of rank in England, in the United States you will be sure to find an association. From that moment, they are a power seen from afar, whose actions serve as an example."[22]

Taxes and the Nonprofit World in America

It was only natural that these associations or committees would adopt the parliamentary process of governance to bring order to their meetings and work toward their goals. As the number of organizations grew, the government saw the need to stimulate the support of these organizations rather than assume the responsibility itself.

The first federal taxes on corporate America were created during the Civil War, with the government specifically taxing railroads, banks, and canal companies. This taxation was expanded in 1894 through an Act of Congress which approved the first general income tax on all corporations.

However, as religious, educational, and charitable institutions were not mentioned in the Act, they were assumed to be exempt. To be certain this understanding was in fact correct, an implicit exemption was then spelled out in a rewrite of the Act itself. However, the 1894 Act was later found to be unconstitutional. It was thus not until after the Sixteenth Amendment to the U.S. Constitution was passed in 1913, which specifically spelled out the Congressional right to assess and collect taxes, that new federal income tax legislation appeared benefiting religious, educational, and charitable institutions. This "tax exemption was granted to groups that relieved the government of having to provide a service—schools, hospitals, social service agencies, and the like. The law limited tax-exempt status to charitable institutions, which received most of their funds from private donors."[23]

The exemption for donating to these organizations was inserted into the tax laws as an exception to the general taxes. In 1917, along with the prospective sharp rise of income taxes connected to World War I, Congress authorized gifts to charitable organizations to be deductible by the donor. After World War I, further changes were made in the tax code and the tax-exempt status of nonprofit organizations (NPOs).[24]

Today, Congress authorizes the operation of several different kinds of nonprofits and delegates their regulation to the Internal Revenue Service (IRS). The IRS defines a *nonprofit corporation* as "an organization formed for the purpose of serving a public or mutual benefit other than the pursuit or accumulation of profits." Thus Congress and the IRS have determined that only specific types of organizations can qualify to be nonprofit or tax-exempt organizations. Finally, the IRS establishes and administers the regulations a nonprofit must follow.

A nonprofit organization that earns more than $5,000 in annual gross receipts must register with the IRS. One that earns $25,000 or more a year must file an annual Form 990, which is an annual report containing financial information.

In giving these corporations tax-exempt status, Congress imposed specific requirements and limitations on their activities. Nonprofit organizations that don't play by the rules risk losing this special status. In particular, no part of the net earnings of nonprofit organizations may benefit any private individuals or stakeholders of the corporation. When a group of individuals and/or board members receives, for their organization, an exemption from paying taxes, the concept of fiduciary duty arises and with it the concept of ethical engagement.

With this insight into the origins of the nonprofit sector in the United States, it would be worthwhile for a small group of people, staff and board, to write a brief history of their organization. This will provide board members, staff and stakeholders with valuable insight into the organization's origin and history, which is the background for understanding its current mission, direct services, governance process, and the unique operational and financial issues it faces. An easy, abbreviated method of conceptualizing the history is to represent it in a time line.

Consider this history within the history and evolution of the nonprofit sector in the United States and within the history of the United States, from the original thirteen colonies to the present.

2

The Role of Government in the Oversight of Nonprofit Organizations

*Democracy is better for us, because the religious sentiment
of the present time accords better with it.*
—Ralph Waldo Emerson

In both the corporate and nonprofit worlds, the role of the governing board is a fiduciary one. According to the *Random House College Dictionary*, a *fiduciary* is "an individual or group of individuals to whom property or power is entrusted for the benefit of another." In the corporate world, the board's responsibility is to the stockholders, but for nonprofit organizations, it is to the stakeholders. A *stakeholder* is an individual who has a vested interest in an organization either as a member, if it is a membership organization, or as an employee, a client, a donor, or a board member. One might argue that because the organization has been granted a tax exemption by the government, the general tax-paying public is also indirectly a stakeholder. In his book, *On Board Leadership*, John Carver states, "every public organization can reasonably be considered a creation of the general public."[1] Instead of stakeholder, another term used is *ownership*. He defines ownership as the "legitimacy base formed by the general public."[2]

Given their unique tax-exempt status, the governing boards of nonprofit organizations have a mandate to act in the interest of the general public. Their legitimacy comes from federal and state governments. In other words, there is some population that, at least in a moral if not legal sense, "owns" the organization. In a membership organization, the concept legitimizes the roles key staff and the governing board play in the operation of the nonprofit, where they have obligations to the members. The members are the owners or stakeholders. In this, "the concept of ownership is narrower than *stakeholder*. Stakeholders can be staff, vendors, neighbors, service recipients and others."[3]

An excellent definition of the purpose of a governing board is Carver's statement that it "is to ensure, on behalf of some ownership, that an organization achieves what it should and avoids that which is unacceptable. That is, the board is accountable for all practices, achievements, and failures of the organization, both of ends and means and both large and small."[4] All boards should internalize this definition.

As the general managing agent, the board must ensure the nonprofit organization acts in accordance with its mission and within both the laws of the state in which it operates and those of the U.S. government. It is because of this fiduciary relationship that both the boards and staffs of nonprofit organizations must perform their duties with absolute integrity. Boards should exercise their authority as a kind of stewardship on behalf of others. However, unfortunately not all do, as there are nonprofit boards that pay little or no attention to their fiduciary, strategic, or visioning responsibilities, let alone to issues of conflict of interest.[4]

Between the years 1989 and 1999, problems arose regarding a number of leaders of nonprofit corporations. The most notable were

Jim Bakker with his religious ministry, William Aramony at the helm of the national office of United Way, and Reverend Bruce Ritter, the CEO of Covenant House in New York City. These cases involved individuals who misappropriated their organization's funds. Then right after 9/11, a number of well-known organizations faced crises of their own creation. The most prominent was the one at the national office of the Red Cross regarding the donations it had received and its provision of services for victims of Hurricane Katrina, as well as an ongoing crisis with its handling of a large portion of the nation's blood supply. This and other cases prompted Congress to start concerning itself with new legislation to oversee the nonprofit sector.

With wanton mismanagement and major accounting crises occurring within Enron, WorldCom, and Tyco Industries, Congress enacted the Sarbanes-Oxley Act of 2002 (SOX) to make corporations more fiscally responsible. The goal of SOX is to strengthen governance in the corporate world and restore investor confidence by ensuring corporate integrity within the management and governance of corporate America.

However, as SOX does not directly focus on the nonprofit sector, many nonprofit board members don't see any relationship between it and the management of their organizations. In fact, there are many individuals sitting on nonprofit boards who do not know what SOX is. In the rich news media environment in which we live, this is surprising. Moreover, while the law has no direct impact on the nonprofit sector, it is having an indirect impact on it. In an attempt to educate the vast segment of individuals serving the nonprofit sector, two major organizations, BoardSource and The Independent Sector, together wrote a monograph entitled, "The Sarbanes-Oxley Act and Implications for Nonprofit Organizations." The focus of it is to educate management and governing boards about the Act's implications. This monograph is available on line at *http://www.independentsector/PDFs/Sarbanes-Oxley.pdf.*

Board members need to examine cases that come to the attention of the public via the media to see what they can learn from them. The American Red Cross situation is well known. Other prominent nonprofit scandals have reached our morning newspapers, including ones involving the American Civil Liberties Union, the James Beard Foundation, and some nonprofit organizations directly linked to Congressmen Tom DeLay and Alan B. Mollohan.

American Red Cross

The most prominent nonprofit organization in the United States may well be the American Red Cross. When we think of the Red Cross, images quickly come to our minds of aiding disaster victims and collecting blood.

Clara Barton and a circle of acquaintances founded the American Red Cross in 1881 to provide relief efforts in natural and manmade disasters, including forest fires, earthquakes, and epidemics. The American Red Cross adopted the mission of the International Red Cross "to help those who suffer, without discrimination whether it be during conflict, in response to natural or manmade disasters, or to alleviate the suffering brought by conditions of chronic poverty."[5] The Red Cross began to provide domestic and overseas disaster relief under the twenty-three years of Barton's leadership.

There are many incidents in which the Red Cross's humanitarian role amply shines. In World War I, it sent a medical "mercy ship" to ports that needed aid. In World War II, the Red Cross helped recruit nursing students and nurses to join the military. It also began to collect blood for the military, which was the beginning of its blood donor program known as the National Blood Donor Service.

The American Red Cross always has been an active participant in providing emergency relief in both small local disasters and major ones, from the 1906 and 1989 San Francisco earthquakes to the devastating storms that have hit the southern coastal areas of our country, including hurricanes Camille, Agnes, Hugo, Katrina, and Rita. The Red Cross also responds to international disasters, including the December 2004 Asian tsunami, the May 2006 Indonesian earthquake, and the August 2006 Lebanese crisis.[6]

The American Red Cross has approximately one thousand chapters and provides a wide range of services, including AIDS education, CPR and first aid classes, and instruction on how to use external defibrillators. In addition, approximately two million people annually learn to swim through its programs while one hundred seventy thousand take its lifesaving exam. Overall, the impact this organization has on American life is enormous.[7]

How does the governance of an organization this size work? The American Red Cross's governing board is comprised of a chairperson and an honorary chairperson, who is always the president of the United States. The president appoints eight individuals to the board while the Red Cross chapters across the United States elect thirty to the board. In addition, the president, CEO, and board members elect twelve individuals as members-at-large. Board members serve three-year terms.

The Red Cross received its charter from Congress in 1900. Since it owes its existence to Congress, the Red Cross is obligated to present Congress with an annual audit compiled by an independent auditing firm. It is not clear as to whether this also requires a management letter from the organization's auditors. Although the Red Cross is a nonprofit organization, it is at the same time a quasi-governmental agency (i.e., it is part of the National Response Plan, which is a federal government plan that manages and coordinates the response to terrorist attacks, major disasters, and other emergencies.[8]) As a 501(c)(3) organization, the Red Cross also submits an annual 990 form to the IRS.

Over the years, the Red Cross has continued doing the work begun by Clara Barton, including eventually taking responsibility for most of America's blood supply. The blood collection program that began with the military in World War II grew into a major program in 1946. "Emboldened by the growing demand for blood and conscious of the need to maintain its prominent role in peace-time, the Red Cross announced its 'National Blood Donor Program,' which was endorsed by the American Medical Association, the American Hospital Association, the U.S. Public Health Service, the Veterans Administration, the Army, and the Navy in 1948."[9] The American Red Cross grew into an exceedingly large organization. Its blood bank business became a multibillion dollar operation. At the same time, this led to a bureaucratic, management, and legal nightmare.

The Red Cross Blood Donor program became the Department of Biomedical Services, which today generates $2-plus billion in revenue and 45 percent of the nation's blood. The blood and blood products are sold to thousands of hospitals and used for a variety of patient services. The Red Cross also entered a "lucrative venture with Baxter Travenol Pharmaceutical … to build a $38 million fractionation plant to manufacture plasma products." The rationale for this venture was that "with its own processing plant, it could double its market share."[10]

All this was happening while the organization was living up to its stated mission of providing disaster relief, but the relief side of the organization was generating considerably less income then medical sciences.

In the summer of 1980, the Center for Disease Control notified the American Red Cross that it was about to publish some statistics in its *Morbidity and Mortality Weekly Report* concerning "what looked like a new illness of potential epidemic proportion, possibly transmitted by blood."[11] It was AIDS. In 1981, an individual blood donor tested HIV positive, but the American Red Cross failed to inform the hospital that collected the blood until four years later.

By 1983, ample evidence supported the conclusion that blood transmitted the AIDS virus. At the same time, Stanford University Hospital discovered a T-cell blood test could determine whether a blood donor was an AIDS carrier. Stanford was "the first in the nation to screen donated blood with a surrogate blood test, in this case the T-cell test. T-cell testing met all the criteria the blood industry claimed to need for a surrogate test. It was highly specific to AIDS, reliable, reproducible, and fast."[12]

Stanford was willing to share the test with the Red Cross and other blood banks, but the FDA's blood industry policies were resistant to change. The Red Cross saw no reason to change its policies until the blood industry developed a new test, which was not until 1985. Interestingly comparative testing showed that Stanford's T-test failed to identify only 0.2 percent of infected donors.

While policy began to change, it did so slowly. The American Red Cross (with its network of fifty-two regional blood centers, an impressive Washington, D.C. headquarters dubbed the "Marble Palace," 2,817 chapters, a multimillion dollar research lab, a closed-circuit TV network, and a production studio) became arrogant. "Its vast reservoir of goodwill enabled it to procure for free millions of units of blood which it converted into a half-billion-dollar commodity,"[13] all tax-exempt. The Red Cross turned a blind eye to the mounting evidence that HIV could be transmitted by blood and blood products, but eventually began to feel the economic consequences of failing to test donors.

The next fifteen years provided many challenges for the American Red Cross. Over these years the governing board chose four individuals to serve as the CEO and president: They were Elizabeth Dole (1991–99), Dr. Bernadine Healy (1999–2001), Marsha J.

Evans (2002–05), and John F. McGuire, who began his tenure as CEO and president in 2006.

In 1991, Elizabeth Dole, a former Secretary of Transportation and Secretary of Labor, became the new CEO and president. She quickly recruited a team of advisors to guide her in all her decision making. At this time, she was confronted with the reality that the nation's blood supply was tainted with Hepatitis B and AIDS. Mrs. Dole spearheaded a $120 million reorganization of the Red Cross's entire blood collection system, changing the odds of a person receiving tainted blood from one in forty thousand to one in one hundred fifty thousand. It was to be one of the most far reaching changes the organization had ever made.[14]

But was it? Her plan was to shut down the blood banks one at a time. Mrs. Dole eventually learned her plan was not feasible. The plan "to shut down the blood banks simply wasn't practical.… The Red Cross wound up not shutting them down, because they couldn't have collected enough blood to make up for the shortfall."[15] It appears that an enormous amount of money was spent with little results.

A year later, the Food and Drug Administration (FDA) found that unsafe blood products were being released,[16] and the Red Cross was failing to protect the blood supply from Hepatitis B and AIDS. To address this problem, the Red Cross "agreed to establish clear lines of managerial control over a newly established quality assurance system in all regions; to enhance training programs; and to improve computer systems, records management, and policies for investigating and reporting problems, including adverse reactions."[17]

At this time Mrs. Dole took a leave of absence to assist her husband, Senator Robert Dole, in his bid for the Republican Party presidential nomination. Mrs. Dole's stand-in, Gene Dyson [interim president appointed by the board], commissioned an internal audit by KPMG Peat Marwick. The report "struck at the heart of Mrs. Dole's leadership, revealing an organization deeply troubled, financially and managerially."[18]

Up through this time, the Red Cross's response to disasters had been consistently good. Most people saw it as a disaster relief organization and a facilitator of needed blood to our local hospitals. However, the reality was that the Red Cross was distributing more than half of the nation's blood supply without this task even being in its charter or mission statement. To handle this responsibility and disaster relief, the Red Cross in 1996 had thirty-two thousand employees and 1.4 million volunteers along with a budget of $1.7 billion. The biomedical division had fourteen thousand employees, including some who were paid more than $200,000 per year.

Bernadine P. Healy, M.D. replaced Elizabeth Dole as the president of the Red Cross in 1999. Dr. Healy led the organization through the September 11, 2001, terrorist attacks and the subsequent collection of donations for victims' families through the Liberty Fund. Unfortunately, the nation eventually learned that not all the money was going to those families. With $500 million raised, the Red Cross decided to use the money for a variety of services, including helping to prepare for future terrorist attacks.

But the 9/11 families, Congress, the media, and eventually the American public became outraged. The concept of diverting $264 million of the $500 million in donations to a rainy day fund for future terrorist attacks was outrageous. To compound things, individuals complained that the Red Cross dispersed cash assistance too slowly and that it did not cooperate with other relief agencies. In addition, Dr. Healy had made an urgent plea for blood for those injured in the attacks, but as it turned out, the blood was not needed. "In the weeks immediately following September 11, blood collections increased 40 percent over collections earlier in 2001. Because only a small amount of blood was needed to treat survivors of the attacks, a nationwide surplus developed, which stressed the collection system.... About five times the usual proportion of units of blood became outdated and had to be discarded in the months following September 11."[19]

After it collected the 9/11 money, the Red Cross was publicly reprimanded. It ultimately agreed to use all of the money for the victims, and among other things promised better accountability. Red Cross holdbacks were also evident after the 1989 earthquake in San Francisco, where it was alleged the Red Cross turned over to victims only ten million dollars of the fifty million dollars raised, keeping the difference for future disasters and organizational expansion.[20]

The Red Cross's management of cash also reflected a lack of sound fiduciary policy. Theft and embezzlement seem to run through the organization's recent history. However, ironically Dr. Healy was criticized by the board for firing the New Jersey Hudson County Chapter's executive director and bookkeeper when she learned they had embezzled almost $2 million.

Dr. Healy resigned in October 2001, indicating that one of the main issues was her aggressive support of Israel's membership in the International Red Cross. Some people called her autocratic and arrogant, while others said she was a "strong woman with a decisive manner who made smart decisions, but even they conceded that she was not always politic.... Paul Clolery, editor of the *Nonprofit Times*, which closely monitors charities said, 'she is hard-driving and she's a tough boss and the organization is in better shape than the mess she inherited.'"[21]

Two months later in December 2001, the "Food and Drug Administration asked a Federal court to hold American Red Cross (ARC) in contempt of a 1993 consent decree covering ARC's blood program. FDA also asked the court for authority to levy prospective fines against ARC for future violations."[22] The FDA's laws and regulations had been created to establish overlapping safeguards for protecting the blood supply, but ten years after they had passed, the Red Cross was still not in compliance. The sixth inspection of the Red Cross's national headquarters between February and April 2000 revealed the following:

- "Incorrect labeling and release of blood potentially contaminated with cytomegalovirus;

- Lack of adequate quarantine and inventory controls;

- Inadequate donor registration controls and failure to maintain accurate and current lists of deferred donors; and

- Erroneous, premature release of computerized 'holds' on blood donations."[23]

Marsha Johnson Evans, a former CEO of the Girl Scouts of America and Navy Admiral, became CEO and president of the American Red Cross in June 2002. Here was a woman with both a reputation for and experience in the leadership of large organizations. She stepped into the continued bloody mess that previous presidents of the organization could not bring to resolution.

Despite this new leadership, the FDA sued the Red Cross again in 2002, and another consent decree was signed in the spring of 2003. Two years later, the Red Cross agreed to sign a revised FDA consent decree. This time the FDA added "a series of clear deadlines" … and addressed "additional types of violations observed after reviewing the results of a 2002 inspection," which included:

- "Numerous and troubling problems in producing blood products"

- "Lack of management control and quality assurance oversight that could lead to a patient receiving potentially unsafe blood"

- Failure "to correct deviations from the previous inspection"

- "Lack of quality assurance oversight"

- "Release of unsuitable products"

- "lack of ARC's inventory control"

- "unknown disposition of blood products"[24]

Then the most disastrous hurricane to ever hit the United States blew into the Louisiana-Mississippi Gulf Coast area in September 2005, destroying its coastal region and much of New Orleans. While the Red Cross had the advantage of being a quasi-governmental agency with a direct relationship to governmental agencies, it wasn't prepared to deal with a disaster of this magnitude tearing through the Gulf region. However, the Red Cross did mobilize more than 244,000 volunteers, provide 3.8 million overnight stays, serve sixty-eight million snacks and meals, and provide financial aid to over one million families.[25]

There were numerous problems with the disaster relief process. It really was an enormous task—one the Red Cross was not prepared to handle, let alone our federal government. To top things off, the Red Cross ended up depleting its Disaster Relief Fund. For the first time in its history, the Red Cross had to take out a loan to cover its disaster relief efforts. Despite this, the Red Cross should be applauded and thanked for what they did accomplish. At the same time, it needs to acknowledge that it did make a number of serious missteps and vow not to make them again.

Criticism of the Red Cross's handling of relief operations for Katrina victims abounded in all media for months after the hurricane's onslaught. Despite the criticism of this area, Marsha Evans must have been aware that the Red Cross was still also having problems with its biomedical division during 2005. All of this undoubtedly led to enormous stress, and she resigned on December 13, 2005.

The next CEO and president of the American Red Cross is John F. Maguire, the former head of its Biomedical Sciences division and blood operations, who was appointed Ms. Evans' immediate successor. In spring 2006, the *Wall Street Journal* noted the Red Cross was still struggling to adhere to federal regulations regarding blood safety. "With little public notice, the Red Cross has paid more than $5 million in fines in the past three years and carried out more than a dozen recalls for violating a 2003 court order that was supposed to clean up the business."[26]

While questions arise concerning the leadership of the three former "CEO-Presidents," the FDA announcement in September 2006 of "an additional $4.2 million fine for failure to meet established blood safety laws" provokes one to wonder why the problems regarding the blood supply still persist under this individual's leadership. How is this issue going to be confronted and solved?[27]

Moreover, besides Katrina and the issues with the biomedical operation, the American Red Cross has had to confront a number of incidents involving embezzlement and theft, including:

- The embezzlement of $2 million in the New Jersey Hudson County chapter

- The theft of $120,000 in a Connecticut chapter

- The theft of debit cards in Texas

- The theft of money by employees of a contractor

- The theft of computers and software

- Internal theft of Red Cross data containing the names of donors, their birthdates, and social security numbers.

It may be that the large size of the organization presents a temptation to others to steal. The national office and the local chapters need to understand their fiduciary responsibilities. Obviously, they need to focus on security. The relationship with the national office and the local chapters must also be clearly defined. The national office ought to have specific criteria that chapters need to meet annually in order to maintain their charter, and in turn be able to participate and vote in the American Red Cross's national convention.

Congress surely will discover this as it investigates the machinations of the Red Cross through the Senate's Select Committee on Finance. The Committee began to discuss this in December 2005 when it "began an inquiry into the American Red Cross ... seeking a broad range of information about its governance, its handling of money for disaster relief and its compensation policies."[28] Senator Charles Grassley, the chairman of the committee, voiced concern that only five members of a fifty-member board were involved in the decision to pressure Ms. Evans to resign, and that there were no available minutes regarding this action. "This most vital of all decisions—the removal of the president of a multibillion dollar organization—was done with only a small number of board members and without a single piece of paper."[29]

Obviously there were also problems at the executive offices. The chairwoman of the board, Ms. McElveen-Hunter, "was more visible at headquarters, spending considerable time in her office there, hiring a staff for herself and taking on more of the daily operations of the organization."[30] Clearly, a board chairperson has no business meddling in the management of an organization unless there is no staff. This certainly is not the case at the American Red Cross.

On the other hand, the dismissal of Marsha Evans, the second high-profile executive to be let go in a short period of time, has to reflect back on the board. What is going on inside the boardroom? Why does the chairwoman have an office and staff inside the Red Cross building? What kind of communication goes on between the board and these CEOs? How can change come about at the Red Cross? To arrive at an answer, we need to recognize that the Red Cross has three inherent problems: its relation to the federal government, its governing process, and its management of day-to-day operations.

As to the first problem, during the past fifteen years it appears the American Red Cross's relationship to the government through its CEOs and members of the governing board has at times been helpful but has at others been disastrous. Hurricane Katrina is a good example of having in theory a working relationship with government agencies, but one which can't be fulfilled effectively. The size of the disaster might be a factor, but perhaps the overall relationship of the Red Cross with Congress and government agencies needs to be reworked.

The way a governing board functions can determine how a non-profit organization does as well. The structure of the Red Cross governing board is cumbersome, as the board itself is too large. Over the past fifteen years, there also appear to have been many conflicts of interest both at the executive and the board levels. For example, if board members are from specific chapters, do they represent the interest of their respective chapters or the national organization? If they represent only the interests of their chapters or regions, how can they perceive the issues that affect a national organization?

Other related questions need to be asked: What is the relationship between local chapters and the national organization? Is the relationship consistent among all the chapters? Do local chapters derive their tax-exempt status from the national organization? Or are they individually incorporated at the local and federal levels?

Congress, the president, and the board individually and collectively are capable of changing the operation of this enormous organization. Initially, it needs to get its governance act in order. This requires four steps. First, the board needs to understand the history of the organization and how it evolved into its current status, as this is crucial for making policy decisions. Second, it must adopt a fiduciary policy that is open to scrutiny. Third, it needs to create a strategic plan that is realistic and achievable within a three-to-five year period, with the staff involved in this process. Finally, within this framework, the board needs to participate in creating the organization's vision. To achieve a vision, the board must engage in discussions of the issues that affect the future of the organization. Clearly, one of the issues that needs to be discussed is: should the biomedical services operation be included in the mission? If the answer is yes, the Red Cross ought to revise its mission statement for there is no mention of the blood program in it. Two possible options are either to sell the operation or set up the blood division as a separate 501(c)(3) organization.

In regards to board decision making—if only a few members of the board are making crucial decisions, those members are usurping the fiduciary responsibilities of the other members. The Red Cross board needs to work at developing consensus and maintaining an ongoing open dialogue with the CEO. Individual board members need to keep in mind that they do not speak for the board as a whole, as only the entire board can give directives to the CEO.

Pending federal legislation may limit the number of individuals who can serve on a nonprofit governing board. This should have a positive impact on the American Red Cross and other large nonprofit organizations that have very large and unwieldy boards of directors.

If the American Red Cross's governing board had adopted a policy of doing a periodic, thorough assessment of the performance of the organization, the current problems may not have occurred. Assessment should have been carried out at four performance levels: CEO, board, management, and organization. Assessment breeds introspection and issue identification, which is good for any organization. Issue identification leads to serious discussions and hopefully to wise decision making. But there is nothing to indicate these processes occurred.

The other factor in the successful operation of a nonprofit organization is the state of its management. The American Red Cross is an organization that requires experienced leadership both in governance and at the senior management level. The CEO must be a skilled leader and a productive manager with a sense of integrity that is shared throughout the management team and the department. The CEO must also be skilled at communicating with the board as a whole and individually with board members. At the same time, the CEO must have managers who have the skills to manage and solve problems within an ethical framework. Managers need to understand the goals and objectives to be attained. The results should be backed up by impeccable metrics. The organizational climate should make everyone feel comfortable about speaking up if there is something wrong. Above all, everyone must be committed to the Red Cross mission and to meeting all government regulations. The end result must be a new American Red Cross rededicated to its mission and committed to operate in an efficient and effective manner.

In terms of how this approach might play out, we should note the current status of the organization. First, "while the 125-year-old nonprofit group is best known for heroic disaster-recovery efforts and its storied service to soldiers in wartime, blood has become its biggest business."[31] Unfortunately, there are still problems in the

Biomedical Division. On the surface, it appears these problems must be management related. However, the fact that they have repeatedly occurred over a fifteen-year period is amazing and shocking at the same time.

Besides the blood problem, the aftermath of Hurricane Katrina is still playing out. The FBI is now involved, looking into the "improprieties in the distribution of millions of dollars' worth of Red Cross relief supplies." Volunteers have made accusations of wrongdoing. "Several Red Cross workers who first raised the issue of possible wrongdoing in the New Orleans operation said that they were not only initially ignored, but also barred from further relief work."[32]

As you think about the American Red Cross, here are some questions that you might want to contemplate: Where are the internal controls? Where are the auditors? Where are the auditors' management letters? Why haven't board members read the management letters and instructed the CEO to enact them and periodically report the status of their completion? If progress is not being made, does the board know the reason? Why aren't the CEO and the managers achieving results? With respect to the recommendations within these letters, why haven't they been acted on?

Here are some questions for the reader to contemplate: If you were CEO/president of the American Red Cross between 1991 and 1999, how would you have responded to the blood problem? What if anything would you have done differently than Dr. Healy? Based on the information you have, what would you have done differently than Marsha Evans? What do you think is happening at the governance level? If you were a member of the board, what issues would you want the board to be focusing on in its deliberations? And what would be your assessment of the Red Cross's situation?

The turnover at the CEO level points to the rocky relations that Red Cross CEOs have with this large a board, let alone the disastrous reverberations that must occur within the organization. How do these filter down within the national office to the biomedical division and then the chapter level? The nature of the work of this organization requires that in addition to its mission, it ought to have a credo that encompasses the values and ethics of a service organization both in the national office and within the communities it serves.

The American Red Cross has addressed the criticism. In a response to the chair of the Senate Finance Committee (Charles Grassley of Iowa), the Red Cross said it was "fully cooperating with the Senate Finance Committee and Chairman Grassley in response to their questions regarding the operations of the American Red Cross. The American Red Cross is committed to learning from our prior challenges and making the necessary changes to improve the delivery of services to the American People.... The Red Cross wants to implement the best corporate governance practices found in the charitable and for-profit sectors.... To that end, the American Red Cross has initiated an independent governance review and will soon host a summit on corporate governance best practices, all with the purpose of developing concrete recommendations."[33]

The Biomedical Services division does not appear to be part of the American Red Cross's mission. However, there is a clear historical trail as to how the Red Cross was asked to take on the responsibility for a good portion of America's blood supply. Despite its being very successful, serious consideration needs to be given to separating Biomedical Services from Disaster and Relief Services. Two distinct nonprofit organizations may need to be created, each with separate missions, governing boards, CEOs, managers, staff, and volunteers. At least, the board acknowledges that it needs to review its process of governance and is scheduled to do so.

"In the NONPROFIT world, one of the basic building blocks of good governance is an independent board of directors that can monitor finances, ask tough questions about policy, and hold man-

agers accountable if things go wrong."[34] This is basically acknowl-
edged by the Red Cross in its February 24, 2006 press release in
which it announced that its board of governors began "a comprehensive assessment of its governance model with the goal of identifying concrete reforms that will streamline the organization's ability
to meet the growing demands of its mission." This commitment,
along with Congressional examination of how the organization
functions, can only strengthen this fine organization.

The American Red Cross is a great and remarkable humanitarian
organization that has been challenged by its size, its urgent role in
responding to the last two catastrophic hurricanes, and its blood
program problems. However, it will survive and be there for all of
us.

American Civil Liberties Union

The next case involves a decision made by the CEO of the American Civil Liberties Union to do research on its donors, which is not
an unusual approach. Nonprofit organizations often do research on
donors and potential donors as it is a common practice in fund-raising. The ACLU entered into a contract with a reputable fund-raising firm to do the research. However, the CEO never consulted
with the board to get its approval. Thus "the group's new data collection practices were implemented without the board's approval or
knowledge and were in violation of the ACLU's privacy policy at
the time."[35]

While a board may give the CEO the authority to sign specific
contracts, it ought not give this individual carte blanche to sign all
contracts. Instead, the board should give the CEO authority to sign
contracts up to a specified amount, with all other contracts to be
reviewed by the board as a whole or by its executive committee.
Contracts and policy decisions are the purview of the board of directors. Obviously, here is a situation of intentional, calculated, or

careless neglect in communicating with the board regarding policy decisions.

The James Beard Foundation

The James Beard Foundation was shaken in 2004 when it was disclosed that hundreds of thousands of dollars had been misused. Although the foundation's former president, Leonard F. Pickell Jr., denied the subsequent theft accusation, apparently the board had known about the situation for months but did nothing about it.[36]

Boards ought to be familiar with their organizations' financial reports. All board members ought to be able to have a reasonable understanding of the information on their organization's balance sheet and operating statement. If they don't, the organization's comptroller or treasurer should use a PowerPoint presentation or overhead projector to clearly convey the prior month's financials.

The financial information should be presented by using a slide-by-slide format, or in the case of the overhead projector, by covering the lines that are yet to be viewed. The object is to make certain everyone understands what is being shown.

With regards to the James Beard Foundation, the key questions are: why wasn't the amount that was missing being recorded in the financials? Why didn't the comptroller or staff accountant recognize that something was wrong? These questions ought to arise with respect to any significant misuse of an organization's funds. Likewise, boards should not allow themselves to become immobilized when a crisis occurs. Instead, they should deliberate in a timely manner and take responsible action. Furthermore, boards need to clarify the values they want to see permeated throughout the organization and align those values with policy.

United States Congressmen

In 2005-06, Congressmen Tom DeLay and Alan B. Mollohan were accused of misusing funds. Congressman DeLay was under investigation for ethics violations, with both he and his foundation (the DeLay Foundation for Kids) being in the headlines for apparent misuse of the foundation's money. In addition, the foundation, which was set up and funded by corporations to help children, has been accused of serving as an entrée for lobbyists by allowing them and their executives to have access to DeLay.

These questions arose in 2005 when the foundation was accused of funding golf trips to Tahiti and Scotland. Since then, DeLay has been indicted in connection with breaking campaign finance laws in Texas. Two of his former aides, one a partner with Washington lobbyist Jack Abramoff, have pleaded guilty to corruption. "Mr. DeLay also was rebuked three times" in 2004 "by the House ethics committee for fund-raising abuses and misuse of government agencies."[37] DeLay has since resigned from Congress.

Federal prosecutors have investigated Congressman Alan B. Mollohan as to whether any federal taxpayer money went to support five nonprofit organizations in West Virginia. Through the use of special spending allocations known as earmarks, he allegedly managed to get $254 million earmarked for these nonprofits.

One of these projects, the Institute for Scientific Research, was his creation: "a glistening glass-and-steel structure with a swimming pool, sauna, and spa rising in a former cow pasture in Fairmont, W.Va., thanks to $103 million of taxpayer money he garnered through special spending allocations known as earmarks. The headquarters building is likely to sit largely empty upon completion ... because the Mollohan-created organization that it was built for, the Institute for Scientific Research, is in disarray, its chief executive, having resigned under a cloud of criticism over his $500,000 annual compensation, also paid by earmarked federal money."[38]

Top employees and board members are friends and former aides who provide Mollohan with steady campaign contributions and enhanced publicity. Mollohan, who had been a member of the House Ethics Committee, resigned from it.[39]

In both these cases, a close relationship existed among the foundation's staff, board, and founders. These arrangements are not limited to a particular political party, as DeLay is a Republican while Mollohan is a Democrat. (There is much more to these cases, so those who are interested can find additional information on the Internet.)

If you spend some time researching the Form 990s of small private foundations, you will find some foundations whose board members receive five-to-six figure payments for performing their fiduciary duties. State attorney generals are beginning to investigate improper self-dealing at foundations that operate within their jurisdictions.

If you are sitting on the board of a foundation or nonprofit organization set up in this fashion, think about what your real obligations are to the organization's real stakeholders. In particular, what are your fiduciary responsibilities?

Here are three regionally based organizations that were confronted with key issues during the past few years. In New Jersey, the New Jersey Symphony Orchestra faced a dilemma regarding a rare gift. Farther up the east coast in New England, the prestigious Groton School was censured for failing to file a report with a state agency, while in Concord, New Hampshire, issues arose regarding the pay and benefits of the rector of St. Paul's School. Let's briefly examine these three cases.

New Jersey Symphony Orchestra

The New Jersey Symphony purchased for its players rare string instruments made by Stradivari, Guarneri, and Guadagnini, purportedly valued at $50 million but actually worth between $15.3 and $26.4 million. Driven by fear of "sabotaging" the deal, the symphony management "deceived their board and the public over the instruments' value."[40] While some board members were aware of the transaction, many others were not informed about it, even though the terms involved the forgiving of a $1 million loan to the orchestra by the owner of the violins. The owner of the violins also donated $1.1 million to the orchestra to be used to purchase the violins. Even those who knew about the situation were not informed as to what they were getting. The donor ended up pleading guilty to tax fraud.[41]

While a committee had been established to review the instruments and make recommendations regarding the purchase, the decision eventually reverted to the CEO and the executive committee. In this situation, there was apparent overt deception, lack of communication, and lack of transparency.[42]

Transparency is paramount in management and board transactions. While it is nice to consider the donor's needs, those needs should not jeopardize the board's or the institution's integrity.

Groton School

The second case involves the Groton School in Groton, Massachusetts. This case goes back to 1999 when a student was apparently abused. The school's management was required by state law to report this to the Massachusetts Department of Social Services. It did not, even though every school management team in the state—be it public, private or religious—knows the Department of Social Services must be notified "within 48 hours of learning that a child has been physically or emotionally abused."[43]

Furthermore, this incident was never reported to the board until the Massachusetts Department of Social Services found out and took the board to court, charging it "with a criminal misdemeanor" for failing "to file a written report" with the department.[44] This example raises questions about the relationship between management and the governing board as it indicates a serious weakness in management's communication with the board. It was management's responsibility to file the report in a timely manner and simultaneously report it to the board. Ultimately, the governing board is responsible for omissions made by the CEO. One of a board's prime responsibilities is to hire a capable and competent CEO who can assume responsibility for the day to day operation of the organization. In this case, the CEO apparently failed. In April 2005, the board was found guilty and was fined $1000.[45] The fine was not exorbitant, but the publicity was not flattering.

St. Paul's School

The third case took place in Concord, New Hampshire. St. Paul's School made the national news when it became known that the rector of the school was being paid an exceedingly high salary, which upset a number of alumni. The board's executive committee had justified the exceedingly large salary package on the basis that the head of the school had raised a lot of money for the school. Despite this, fund-raising goals were not being met. State tax authorities began an investigation. The notoriety and concern of the alumni created sufficient uproar so that the rector retired earlier than he had planned.[46]

With examples like these coming to the attention of state legislatures and Congress, is it any wonder they have begun to consider legislation that would tighten the controls on nonprofits? In fact, in Massachusetts and New York, new legislation regarding the operations of nonprofit organizations is working its way through the legislatures.

Given these cases of nonprofit malfeasance in earlier years and of new nonprofit problems coming to the forefront, it is only a matter of time before other states follow, especially since hardly a month or sometimes even a week goes by without a nonprofit being spotlighted in the newspapers. Therefore, CEOs and governing boards are advised to check with their state attorney general's office for information on pending legislation regarding nonprofits operating in their state.

At the federal level, the Senate Select Committee on Finance is also moving ahead on proposed legislation. This committee held hearings on June 22 and July 22, 2004, on *Charity Oversight and Reform: Keeping Bad Things from Happening to Good Charities*. Senator Chuck Grassley, chairman of the Committee on Finance, set the tone: "It's obvious from the abuses we see that there's been no check on charities. Big money, tax free, and no oversight created a cesspool in too many cases."[47]

Committee staff drafted legislation and collected input from interested parties. With proposed legislation potentially moving on to the hot burner, the Sarbanes-Oxley Act provides the perfect forum for nonprofit boards to focus on the implications for their organizations. This analysis ought to concentrate on board practices and methods of operation. Boards and their chief executive officers ought to look at the federal proposals to see how they may impact their organizations.

A discussion draft released by the Senate Select Committee on Finance reflects proposals for reforms and best practices for tax-exempt organizations. These have been passed on to the Senate. If it had not been for other urgent business coming before Congress, these proposals would have been voted on before the end of 2005.

Let's look now at some of these recommendations. While many focus on financial accountability, they also turn attention to management, planning, and measurement of outcomes:

On every fifth anniversary of the IRS's determination of the tax-exempt status of an organization that is required to apply for such status, the organization would be required to file with the IRS such information as would enable the IRS to determine whether the organization continues to be organized and operated exclusively for an exempt purpose (i.e., whether the original determination letter should remain in effect.) Information to be filed would include current articles of incorporation and by-laws, conflict of interest policies, evidence of accreditation, management policies regarding best practices, a detailed narrative about the organization's practices, and financial statements. Such information would be made publicly available. The IRS would not be required to issue a new determination letter (or to review all organizations), but would be permitted to revoke tax-exempt status if a review undertaken by the IRS concluded that the organization was no longer entitled to exemption. Failure to file the five year review would result in loss of tax exempt status. A sliding scale processing fee would be charged of all filers by IRS/EO to cover all costs of the reviews performed.[48]

New rules would also apply to donor advised funds (DAF). Included in the proposal would be requirements that DAFs secure from the donor an acknowledgement that grants will not convey a private benefit to the donor. The rules would also require a minimum threshold of activity of DAFs. When donations are made to international organizations, the organization would have to be on the IRS-published list of foreign organizations.

Self-dealing rules would also be applied to non-profit organizations:

Under present law, excise taxes apply if private foundations engage in acts of self-dealing with disqualified persons. Self-dealing transactions generally include the sale, exchange, or leasing of property, the lending of money or other extension of credit; the furnishing of goods, services or facilities; payment of unreasonable compensation by a private foundation; transfer to or use by a disqualified person of a private foundation's income or assets; and certain payments to government officials. With the exception of the payment of unreasonable compensation, these rules would be extended to public charities (and social welfare organizations) so that, in general, self-dealing transactions between a public charity (or social welfare organization) and a disqualified person would result in excise taxes. In general, the definition of disqualified person for purposes of the private foundation rules would be adopted for public charities, except that adjustments would be made to include persons with substantial influence over the organization, and the rules would be modified as necessary to take into account relationships with affiliated or supporting entities.[49]

Here are some additional recommendations from the Senate Finance Committee's staff:

- Private foundations would be prevented from making donations to donor advised funds.

- Charities would have to use the applicable U.S. government rate for paying for travel expenses. Penalties would be assessed for noncompliance.

- States would be given the authority to pursue certain Federal tax law violations.

- Reforms will be forthcoming "to ensure accurate, complete, timely, consistent, and informative reporting by tax-exempt organizations."

- Chief executive officers of tax-exempt organizations will have to sign a declaration under penalty of perjury certifying that they have in place processes and procedures to ensure that the federal information returns and tax returns are accurate and comply with the IRS code.

- Penalties for failure to file required information as well as Form 990 will increase significantly.

- The IRS may require all information to be filed electronically.

- Tax-exempt organizations with gross revenue of over $250,000 will require an independent audit of the organization's financial statements.

- Any affiliations to other tax-exempt organizations will have to be listed on a chart.

- Organizations with over $250,000 in gross revenue will also be required to provide a detailed description of the organization's annual performance goals and measurements for meeting those goals (to be established by the board of directors) for the past year and goals for the coming year. The purpose of this requirement is to assist donors in better determining an organization's accomplishments and goals when deciding whether to donate rather than it being a point of review by the IRS.

- Organizations that do not file Form 990 because their gross receipts are less than $25,000 will now have to file an annual notification with the IRS. The form, which will have to be filed electronically, will ask for the organization's legal name, any other business name, mailing and web addresses, taxpayer identification number, name of the principal officer, and evidence that gross receipts are less than $25,000. Failure to file for three consecutive years will result in revocation of tax-exempt status.

- Tax-exempt organizations will be required to disclose to the public their financial statements and to post such information on their Web sites.

- Federal liability for board members who breach their fiduciary responsibilities will be established.

Additional suggested requirements of the board are to:

- Establish organizational and management policies.

- Establish, review, and approve program objectives and performance measures.

- Review and approve the auditing and accounting principles and practices used in preparing the organization's financial statements as well as retaining and replacing the organization's auditor. The auditor can be retained for no more than five years.

- Review and approve the organization's budget and financial objectives as well as significant investments and business transactions.

- Oversee the conduct of the corporation's business and evaluate whether the business is being properly managed.

- Establish a conflict of interest policy and create a summary of conflict of interest determinations, both to be attached to the organization's Form 990.

- Establish and oversee a compliance program to address regulatory and liability concerns.

These proposed regulations also focus on board composition and performance. Exempt organizations would be required to report how often they met (and how often they did so without the CEO.) Boards can be no smaller than three members and no larger than fifteen. Board members and prospective board members convicted of a crime would be prohibited from serving on any board for a period of five years.[50] Finally, the IRS "would have the authority to remove any board member, officer, or employee of an exempt organization who has been found to have violated self-dealing rules, conflicts of interest, excess benefit transaction rules, private inurnment rules, or charitable solicitation laws. An organization that knowingly retained a person who is not permitted to serve would lose tax-exempt status or be subject to a lesser penalty."[51]

This Senate report suggests that Congress provide an allocation of ten million dollars for the IRS to support accreditation of charities. "The IRS would have the authority to contract with tax exempt organizations that would create and manage an accreditation program to establish best practices and give accreditation" to organizations that meet best practices. These accreditation programs would review organizations on an ongoing basis for compliance.[52]

Testimony before the Select Finance Committee included that of Diana Aviv, president of the Independent Sector (a national coalition of nonprofit organizations), and former Harvard University president Derek Bok, faculty chair of the Hauser Center for Nonprofit Organizations at Harvard University. In her comments, Diana Aviv said, "preventing, discouraging and eliminating unethical and illegal practices within the voluntary sector will require a multifaceted approach that depends upon the involvement of both government and the voluntary sector." She went on to warn that "it is important that corrective efforts do not produce outcomes that might stifle the great American tradition of giving and of volunteering."[53]

Derek Bok raised concerns as to how regulations would affect small nonprofit organizations. He noted a "burden" would be "imposed on countless tiny local nonprofits with amateur part-time executives and boards composed of neighborhood volunteers." He went on to say, "while supporting the effort to strengthen the accountability of non-profit organizations, I would urge great care in approaching this complex and unfamiliar task. Instead of attempting the difficult feat of crafting model procedures in an effort to encourage optimum performance, or giving the IRS the vast, uncharted task of developing (directly or indirectly) standards for accrediting all nonprofits, I would begin by concentrating on curbing reasonably clear abuses."[54]

Despite the concerns Derek Bok raised, many of the staff recommendations are doable. Organizations, no matter how small, need to learn to set goals and objectives, tracking how well they are being attained. If there were no guidelines for the nonprofit sector to follow, the nonprofit sector might declare it didn't know how to act. However, guidelines do exist. The Model Nonprofit Corporation Act of 1987 describes two basic categories of duty for board members and the senior management team: the duty of care and duty of loyalty. Web-based references to this Act can be found at *http://www.muridae.com/legalbasis.html*, which is an online compendium of federal and state regulations for U.S. nonprofit organizations. (See also commentary at *http://www.ucalgary.ca.*) Among the responsibilities within duty of care are "being informed as to data relevant to board decisions, monitoring the organization's activities, assessing the efficiency of the organizational structure, and providing for both short-term and long-term planning."[55]

Additional information can be found at the Web site of the National Association of Nonprofit Boards, *http://www. boardsource.com.* The association offers an assortment of books and pamphlets that provide guidance to board members. Other resources can be found using Web search engines. For example, the National Association of College and University Business Officers and the National Association of Fundraising Professionals maintain websites and hold conferences at which board members can broaden their knowledge in these areas. Their respective websites are: *http://nacubo.org* and *http://www.afpnet.org.*

3

A Board Member's Guide to Fiduciary Responsibilities

The spirit of the thing lies in the details.
—Mies van der Rohe

When governance and management teams have an understanding of the breadth of the nonprofit sector in the United States and the way it came about as well as insight into some of the legislation aimed at making the nonprofit sector more accountable, it is appropriate they also gain some perspective of what is required of functioning boards. Fulfillment of fiduciary responsibilities is of prime importance.

As defined earlier in chapter 2, a fiduciary is a person or persons to whom property or power is entrusted for the benefit of another.[1] Fiduciary responsibilities are more than being entrusted with protecting all the assets (tangible and intangible) of the nonprofit organization as they also involve making sure those assets are available to both current and future generations.

The fiduciary duties of governing boards are made up of thirteen key elements:

- Attend and participate in meetings

- Apply *Robert's Rules of Order* to board meetings

- Become knowledgeable about the organization

- Hire and annually evaluate the CEO

- Support and practice open communication and transparency

- Support an organizational structure that ensures fiscal strength and security

- Review financial reports and participate in financial management and planning, seeking help when necessary to fully understand the financial information at hand

- Support a conflict of interest policy

- Select auditors, review their report, and act on their recommendations

- Review and understand all contracts and their implications

- Maintain and support due process for employees

- Support and participate in fundraising

- Support and participate in a program to bring diversity to the organization

This view of the board's fiduciary role encompasses more than just protecting the organization's assets. Let's explore these elements.

Attend and Participate in Meetings

No board can function without its members' participation, as attendance is crucial to its functioning. Individuals who can't attend ought if possible be given the opportunity to participate by other means. For example, a board member who is out of town may be able to attend a meeting over a speakerphone. There also are telephone networks that allow one or more board members who are away to participate in a conference call system and be connected to the board meeting.

The telephone, the computer, and the Internet are important adjuncts to the U.S. Postal Service and overnight delivery services. All expand the confines of the boardroom. The Internet also provides opportunities to create board chat rooms or to share documents and broadens the array of communication vehicles.

Boards need to amend their bylaws to include the above items as a legal means for conducting the business of the organization. No board wants to be challenged about the way it is conducting its business. Boards should set this as a priority and periodically review their bylaws to make sure they are carrying on the business of the nonprofit corporation in an efficient and satisfactory manner.

Boards must take responsibility for perpetuating themselves by taking the following steps: Select the right potential board members, people who will challenge the CEO and other senior executives. Orient new board members by arranging face-to-face meetings with all top executives. Assign current board members to be mentors to them. Provide briefing books and site visits while factoring in time to build relationships. Finally, focus on training them—and then train them some more.

Additional steps include: Make sure only board members with independent minds recruit new members. Involve the CEO in the recruiting process, but remember that "most boards would fire their CEOs for filling staff positions as haphazardly as the board recruits for board positions. Selecting board members is much like choosing a finance officer, dentist, or auto mechanic."[2] Therefore, do it wisely.

Board membership requires time, as board members need time to prepare for meetings and to discuss the issues. They must schedule time to absorb information, reflect on it, and make decisions. Members of the board also need time to develop relationships with their colleagues. The board can help by providing social time, such as serving a light meal before a meeting begins. Organize a cocktail party or dinner for the directors and their significant others. Make it attractive enough that members will be motivated to come early.

Apply *Robert's Rules of Order* to Board Meetings.

The bylaws ought to state that meetings will be held using *Robert's Rules of Order*. An abbreviated version, *Robert's Rules of Order Newly Revised In Brief*, is available at most book stores. The rigor by which these rules are adopted ought to be determined by the size and complexity of the organization. The chair should use the rules judiciously, but to paraphrase Henry M. Robert, in a country where most individuals belong to one or more organizations, some understanding of parliamentary procedure ought to be part of one's education. Anyone with an hour to spare can read the first six chapters in the abbreviated version.[3]

Become Knowledgeable about the Organization

To be an effective board member, you need to know the organization. Familiarize yourself with the organization's history and its mission, what it accomplishes, its financial situation, and its strategic plan. Find time to meet its staff, from the bookkeeper to the CEO. Learn how the organization works. Look for opportunities to meet clients and find out what they are gaining from their relationship with the organization. If possible, find time to volunteer in addition to your board service.

Hire and Annually Evaluate the CEO

It is the board's responsibility to hire and annually evaluate the Chief Executive Officer. Evaluations should be done in a timely and professional manner. Because as Daniel Goleman states, "leadership is intrinsically stressful," governing boards need to hire CEOs who value teamwork.[4] Look for self-confident CEO-level candidates who can engage in real debate without dragging in their egos. Integrity, managerial skills, and passionate commitment to the mission of the organization should be foremost in everyone's mind during the assessment and interview processes. In assessing the competency of a candidate to lead your organization, check out the eighteen leadership competences listed in Daniel Goleman et al.'s *Primal Leadership*.

It is important to establish a tone of collegiality. CEOs and directors must work at creating a culture of listening to each other and to others. Make time to meet with the CEO outside of board and committee meetings.

As John Carver points out, it is the CEO who reports to the board. As the CEO is the recipient of all executive authority passed into the operating organization, this authority ought to be clearly stated. Because the board holds the CEO accountable for organizational performance, it must provide direction to this individual in such a way as to preserve board accountability while maximizing CEO flexibility, creativity, and freedom. At the same time, members of the board should have reasonable access to the management and its principal advisors/consultants such as its auditor.[5]

Setting guidelines and responsibilities for the CEO is important. The CEO's relationship and responsibilities with respect to the board ought to be clearly articulated in the job description. However, "it is best that the board as a whole only govern (never advise), while individual board members advise if they wish (but never govern). In other words, the CEO can use board members as advisors *when the CEO chooses to do* so and only as individuals, never as a body." The CEO does not work for individual board members; the CEO works for the entire board. "It is possible with sufficient discipline to keep the respective hats separate."[6]

Finally, boards need to meet periodically without the CEO. These sessions provide board members an opportunity "as peers, to be self-aware and self-critical," in which they ask the right questions about their performance as a group and individually. In these sessions, "social capital facilitates the process and offers boards a new and powerful resource to instill a keener sense of mutual obligation, a custom of critical inquiry, and a culture of accountability and productivity."[7]

Support and Practice Open Communication and Transparency

There must be open communication both among board members and between the board and the CEO. The board should make transparency a top priority, with *transparency* meaning frank, open, and candid communications. Organizations that fail to practice transparency are setting themselves up for an unexpected incident to hurt their reputation and possibly create a serious legal issue. Inform, communicate, and deliver relevant information early and in multiple formats. Make sure meetings focus on substantive issues and policy development, then leave time on the agenda for open discussion.

Support an Organizational Structure that Ensures Fiscal Strength and Security

Besides hiring the CEO, the board should ratify the CEO's choice for head of finances. Organizations with an operating budget of approximately one million dollars ought to have a full-time bookkeeper supervised by the treasurer. Organizations with operating budgets of approximately two million dollars or more ought to have a bookkeeper or staff accountant and a comptroller.

Review Financial Reports and Participate in Financial Management and Planning

While questions exist regarding financial accountability in the corporate world, there also is the same concern about the nonprofit sector. One cannot make crucial decisions without accurate financial data. Recent corporate scandals have focused attention on many corporate activities. A number of corporations have manipulated their accounting, while others have paid their CEOs questionable salaries and benefit packages. This also happens in the nonprofit sector!

Financial accountability can only be achieved if each and every board member understands the nonprofit's balance sheets and operating statements. Unfortunately, most boards have only a few members who understand accounting and know how to read financial statements. This needs to change, as board members are stewards of the "funds with which your organization has been entrusted. The relationship between your organization, its financial supporters, and society as a whole, is a relationship based on trust, not commerce."[8] Because donor contributions are critical to fulfilling the mission of nonprofit organizations, accounting expertise is essential in preserving public trust.

Crucial decisions are often made within the context of financial management. While the board may hire staff to handle the accounting and monitor the budget, it bears ultimate management and oversight responsibility. Members of a board who have little or no understanding of financial reporting should be given an opportunity to learn. The goal should be to have every board member have a basic understanding of the essential concepts of accounting. One of the best ways to train board members in finance is to have each board member who doesn't have accounting in his or her background take a brief tutorial in basic accounting. This can be achieved by using a basic accounting text in a self-directed learning format.

One of the best examples of this is a programmed text used at Harvard Business School in an accounting course for non-financial executives: *Essentials of Accounting* by Robert N. Anthony and Leslie K. Pearlman. As the authors state, "this book will help you teach yourself the essentials of accounting. You will learn what accounting information can—and cannot—tell you about an organization."[9] The book consists of frames that ask the reader to do some task, such as answer a question, make a calculation, or fill in the blanks. The frames are not quizzes; rather each frame represents a learning-by-doing process. Most people should be able to complete most, if not all, frames without difficulty.

By mastering the basics of accounting, board members will begin to understand what is being reported on the organization's operating statement and balance sheet. Most importantly, they will be able to set internal controls, ask intelligent questions, and make intelligent decisions. By taking the initiative in understanding the financials, board members will be able to tie the results to the outcomes they approved in the prior budgeting process.

For understanding the intricacies of financial planning in the nonprofit arena, board members should read Jody Blazek's book,

Financial Planning for Nonprofit Organizations. It provides an excellent discussion of financial planning and budgeting (among other issues) that should be of interest to governing boards, including a thorough "Board Member's Checklist of Fiduciary Duties."[10]

In the end, the board is responsible for making sure that internal controls exist. "Internal controls are those mechanisms that are in place to either prevent errors from entering the process or detecting errors once they have."[11] These internal controls usually are established by the financial management team subject to the input of the board, the finance committee, and the audit committee. For those organizations that have small boards, the finance committee can also assume the role of the audit committee. In addition, the organization's auditors are a valuable resource for good input to internal controls. When the auditor completes an audit, the governing board should insist the auditor provide a management letter outlining any issues the governing body needs to address.

Boards also need to establish a policy for records retention. While the accounting department should provide guidelines as to retaining financial data, this needs to be translated into policy. The policy needs to cover not only financial records but also data, non-financial records, and correspondence—including information on computers.

Support a Conflict of Interest Policy and Code of Ethics

Every board must have a conflict of interest policy. A *conflict of interest* is a situation in which a board member or senior executive encourages or makes a decision that affects the financial interests or political actions of the organization, but which in turn will also benefit the member individually or the member's friend, relative, or business. At least once a year after the annual meeting, every board member, the CEO, and any other senior executives should state for the record if they have any conflict of interest in serving the organization. Thus all conflicts of interest should be identified and stated for the record. Some states such as New Hampshire require that conflicts of interest above a certain dollar value also be published in a local newspaper.

In conjunction with the conflict of interest policy, the board should adopt a code of ethics, then publicly announce the adoption by its staff and board. But where should an organization start on this? One can look to corporate governance practices worth copying.

First, every organization ought to have a credo that states its standard of integrity. It must be clearly articulated and available to its staff, board, and all of its constituencies. This requires "a review of all written codes of conduct, ethics policies, reporting procedures and compliance programs. It is important to target practices and areas that are candidates for questionable integrity practices—such as selection," as well as lobbying, if any, and compensation plans.[12]

Let's look at an unusual example in the corporate world. Good corporate practices begin with creating a climate of integrity. "The corporate world has spoken loudly about the importance of self-governance but very softly, if at all, about standards of corporate integrity. We require integrity standards of almost every profession—think of the medical and legal professions—that aspire to self-governance as a condition of allowing them some interdependence from legal regulation."[13] Here is an example from the corporate world—Johnson & Johnson's Credo:

- "We believe our first responsibility is to the doctors, nurses and patients, to mothers and fathers and all others who use our products."

- "We are responsible to our employees, the men and women who work with us throughout the world."

- "We are responsible to the communities in which we live and work and to the world community as well."

- "Our final responsibility is to our stockholders."[14]

Create an organizational credo of values for your entire organization, remembering that integrity begins with the board, the CEO, and the rest of the staff.

Select Auditors and Review their Report

It is the board's responsibility to retain an auditor to annually review the financial records. The Finance Committee usually interviews prospective auditors and makes recommendations to the board. When hiring auditors, it is best to interview at least three firms, and ideally five. Any firm that does not have experience with nonprofit organizations should be avoided.

Some thirty years ago, the board of directors at the Mount Herman Schools in Northfield, Massachusetts made a decision to change auditors every five years. Their goal was to get a fresh perspective. At an annual meeting of independent school business managers, the school's treasurer recommended that their institutions follow suit. This will soon be mandated in the new federal rules being proposed by the Senate Select Committee on Finance.

If there is a complete audit, the auditors should review the final draft with the board. As noted above, the board should insist the auditors provide a management letter outlining what steps (if any) need to be taken to shore up the fiduciary and financial management of the organization. For those organizations that will not meet the federal guidelines for audits, selection of an independent accountant to review the accounting and financial records is an important task for the board or its finance committee.

In filing the required reports with the IRS and state government agencies, the board should have the CEO and Chief Financial

Officer publicly attest to the accuracy, completeness, and fairness of the financial statements, as well as to the adequacy of the internal accounting controls. The auditors should ask the same of the staff accountant. If the board is large enough, make sure there is an audit committee.

If the auditor is just ascertaining the accuracy of financial statements, it will be impossible within the scope of this kind of task to provide an analysis of the organization's accounting controls. In the past the IRS, as well as many states, required audits for organizations with an operating budget of $100,000 or more. This has changed and now varies by state; for example, in Massachusetts, the threshold is $500,000. Federal legislation may even raise this amount. Boards will have to make crucial decisions if they are exempted, as auditing service prices are high. For example, an accountant's review of financial statements of a small organization with an operating budget of approximately $100,000 to $200,000 can cost as much as $3,000, while an audit for the same organization might cost $6,000 to $8,000. "Creating good internal controls by monitoring them and reporting results to the board are good business practices that can lead to a more ethically run" organization.[15] With an understanding of the accounting process, board members can "be vigilant in protecting themselves against board actions that might lead to fiscal liability."[16]

Review and Understand all Contracts and their Implications

Unless explicit authority is given to the CEO to sign a specific contract, the board should review and approve all contracts. Where deemed appropriate, the organization's counsel should also review contracts. An alternative may be for the board to consider allowing the CEO to execute agreements under a specified dollar value.

Maintain and Support Due Process for Employees

It is the board's responsibility to make sure it has a process for employees to report complaints without fear of reprisals. However, it is important for the board not to allow employees to misuse this opportunity to communicate with board members. Politics and jockeying for promotions do occur within the nonprofit sector as well as the corporate world, and the opportunity to undermine the CEO always exists. The board needs to think how it is going to weigh this information judiciously.

Additional Thoughts Regarding the Board's Fiduciary Role

It is important to establish a tradition of continual improvement. Directors should examine and refine practices as do other professional teams. Besides evaluating the performance of the CEO, the board should examine its own performance as a whole and individually. Boards should also annually review the organization's programs with a focus on measured outcomes.

"Attention to financial discipline, informed oversight, mission fidelity, and primacy of organizational interest are recognized in the law as the board's *duties of loyalty and care*. It is the fundamental work of trusteeship."[17] By fulfilling their fiduciary roles, the board and CEO will be on their way to restoring the trust and confidence of donors, staff, and regulators.

As a nation, our charitable and educational organizations, boards, CEOs, and staff have an obligation to fulfill their fiduciary obligations and avoid all conflicts of interest. "Accountability is the watch word of the day, and it requires that compliance and performance go hand in hand. In a world filled with nonprofits struggling for survival and newspaper reports of governance gaffs, engaged boards are the chief executive's allies—dedicated to the mission,

knowledgeable about the organization's goals and finances, committed to securing the necessary resources, and capable of representing
the organization's goals and finances, committed to securing the
financial resources, and capable of representing the organization in
the community."[18]

4

A Fiduciary Addendum: The Board's Role in Fundraising and Diversity

The gratification of wealth is not its mere possession, but its wise application.
—Cervantes

Fund-raising and diversity are often thought of as lying outside the domain of the board's fiduciary role. Perhaps they have been treated that way in the past, but from today onward, we will think of them as part of the board's support of fiduciary responsibilities.

Support and Participate in Fundraising

Philanthropy is not a modern concept. Private giving is an ancient tradition with clear roots in *western* civilization. Philanthropy comes from the Greek words *philos* meaning love and *anthropos* meaning man, while the Latin word *philanthropia* means benevolence. As an example, in 386 BC when Plato's Academy was founded in Greece, the King of Syracuse made the first major gift, and Cimeon funded the capital improvements to the grounds, laying out the first quadrangle whose design is now reflected on university campuses.

Jumping many centuries toward the end of the fourteenth century, the poem "The Vision of Piers Plowman" advised merchants what to do with their profits, as follows:

> But use ye your winnings to rebuild almshouses,
> To maintain the scholar, to help the stricken,
> To dower girls, or make them nuns,
> To build the broken bridge, and mend the bad road,
> To help the monks, and make rents reasonable,
> And I will send you Michael my archangel.
> And never a fiend shall frighten you or harm you at your death;
> For I will save you from all your despair,
> And bring your souls in safety to my saints in joy.

There is a connection between this poem and the Statute of Uses, adopted in 1601, which is the legal basis for charity in England.[1]

The Industrial Revolution in England wrought much expansion and brought about a secular interest in the welfare of the citizens. Voluntary organizations sprang up to deal with the problems and social issues that were not being solved by the government. In turn, citizens provided for the health, welfare, and education of the needy.

"These ideas and practices crossed the Atlantic with the early settlers and became deeply entrenched here in the Colonial period. Long before the federal government got into the question of tax exemption, the states held that these activities deserved, demanded, and should receive public encouragement in whatever way was feasible through tax legislation and otherwise."[2] An early example was the property of Harvard College, which in the eighteenth century was exempt from paying taxes as was the property of the faculty and students.[3]

While the government provides us with tax-exempt status for our organizations and tax reduction incentives for the donors, fundraising doesn't happen without volunteers. Along with every board of directors, the key volunteers have the responsibility of ensuring there is adequate funding for their nonprofit organization's programs and overhead. The size of the organization and the stage of its development dictate whether fundraising staff is hired. Regardless, every board must take ownership of the fundraising.

One often hears the comment that the ideal board member ought to have the commitment to work, wisdom to share, and wealth to give. The reality is that work and wisdom are essential, but wealth is an ideal. However, the commitment to give to the best of one's ability and to participate in fundraising are equally essential.

"Board leadership and participation are essential to successful fundraising. Raising money also requires a great deal of work and a true partnership between board members and key staff. Board roles are multifaceted—they serve not only as strategists and policy makers, but also as individual solicitors. As board members attempt to ensure that the organization has sufficient resources to implement its mission, their personal involvement in fundraising becomes critical."[4]

"Among the various responsibilities of the board, none is more important than ensuring that the organization has adequate resources to remain financially viable."[5]

"Understanding the nature of charitable giving … is indispensable to a board member's ability to raise money. Philanthropy is not a strange or foreign concept, but a basic dimension of our democratic heritage."[6]

One of the best board training materials for fundraising is *Fearless Fundraising for Nonprofit Boards* published by BoardSource. It is an easy-to-read booklet containing numerous training tools that is accompanied by a video with the same name, "Fearless Fundraising." Information about it and other materials from the National Association of Nonprofit Boards, now known as BoardSource, can be found at *http:/www.BoardSource.org*.

While the board must take ownership of fundraising, it also needs to take advantage of the fund-raising skills of the CEO. If the board hires an individual with fundraising skills, it needs to make sure that person assumes along with the board the leadership in this area. This means the CEO will have to set aside a percentage of his or her time to pursue major gifts. Boards should consider the individual's success in this area when performing the annual performance evaluation.

Charities need to restore the trust and confidence of the donors, the public, and the regulators in their financial competence and integrity. As previously noted, beginning with problems involving the delivery of charitable donations intended for victims of September 11, 2001, an increasing number of cases of mismanagement and abuse of charitable assets by charity managers, officers, directors, and trustees have come to light.

In many instances officers, directors, and trustees are learning about financial problems within their organizations too late to address them in an adequate or efficient manner. Unfortunately, instances also abound in which charity leaders are pocketing assets for their own financial gain. While such abuses can be addressed in part through enhanced education of charity leaders, strong accounting controls, and stepped-up enforcement measures, we need legislation that requires public charities to increase their financial integrity while holding charity leaders to clear standards of accountability.

Some problems arise when in an effort to make fundraising returns look good, executive directors or campaign chairs connive with individual board members or volunteers about how they will regard a gift. For example, an executive director might instruct staff to record a restricted gift or an addition to a donor advised fund as a gift to the annual fund. There are probably many more obfuscated arrangements within boards and between CEOs and board members, none of which should be tolerated.

Support and Participate in a Program to Bring Diversity to the Organization

During the past fifteen years there has been considerable focus on creating diversity within the nonprofit community. As diversity within an organization is important, diversity within the governing body is equally so. Governance should represent the ownership. "Representing the ownership, requires that a board represent diversity within the ownership.

The moral imperative for diversity in board life derives, not from some abstract commitment to humanity, but from the simple fact that responsible action is impossible unless the diversity present in the ownership is integrated into governance."[7]

We live in a diverse society and our nonprofit organizations often serve diverse populations. Boards need to work to attract potential board members with different racial and ethnic backgrounds. Most boards are "lily white" in background, but the clientele served by the nonprofit is usually diverse. Board members whose racial and ethnic backgrounds are similar to the population served will be able to share insights about which a homogeneous group would most likely never have an inkling.

What boards fail to recognize is that there is a wealth of talent within the minority community. Board members fail in looking at governance issues from the minority members' point of view. "Achieving diversity in any sphere of American life is controversial at best. Ironically, there is quite possibly no more divisive issue in

America today than inclusiveness. Nonprofit organizations are not immune to the challenges of this issue, and most often boardrooms of nonprofit organizations are the last places in which the sector has been able to achieve sustainable diversity."[8]

Diversity represents our roots, our present, and our future. "Large numbers of immigrants to the United States have added to the changing face of America." They are still changing it. This diversity presents an enormous opportunity. "Our culture is able to draw from a rich pool of diverse individuals who can enhance work environments by redefining markets, products, strategies, missions, and business practices. Diversity, when used as a business asset can lead to increased productivity and increased market shares."[9]

Despite the great strides that minority groups have made in the United States since the end of World War II, and despite the significant increase in the minority population, a majority of nonprofit organizations do not have racially diverse governing boards. Notwithstanding this reality, there is an increase in boards that have become "racially diverse." Some of this is due to the pressures that have been put on nonprofits "to increase their diversity. Increasingly, demographic and racial diversity are seen as very important, both politically and operationally for boards."[10]

On the other hand, there is still much to achieve. "A May 2002 Booz Allen Hamilton survey showed that boards are facing a dire recruitment scenario. Nearly 1.8 million board seats become available each year, adding to the backlog of 1.2 million standing openings, the survey notes. Minorities are particularly underrepresented on boards, accounting for only 14% of board members as compared with 27% of the population."[11]

Some organizations are very successful at attracting minorities to serve on their boards. Other organizations have tried to attract minorities, but have been unsuccessful. Some attracted a single minority and then found themselves being accused of tokenism by

that member. In this last situation, the accuser wants a more concerted effort to be made to attract other minorities to the board,
while the board wants to get on with the business at hand. The particular board member feels the rest of the board does not recognize
the problem and starts to drop off in attendance, eventually drop-
ping out. The seeking of minority board candidates is quietly rele-
gated to the back burner, and the effort to recruit potential board
members with diverse backgrounds becomes passive.

In scrutinizing the diversity of governing boards, we certainly
need to actively look toward bringing minorities on board. At the
same time, we need to broaden our concept of diversity in a multi-
dimensional way. After all, is it even possible to represent all segments of the diversity continuum on a board? "The entire range of
diversity can be accommodated only by swelling the board to
unmanageable size."[12]The answer is to constitute the board to be a
reflection of its constituencies, giving attention to racial, gender,
religious, age, and geographical characteristics as much as possible.[13]

"Diversity in board composition is, minimally, reflected through
age, gender, socioeconomic status, sexual orientation, physical abili-
ties, religion, skill sets and yes, race. In other words, diversity is not
only an issue of race."[14] To achieve true diversity on nonprofit
boards, there must be a continuous, concerted effort to make diversity recruitment a top priority. This effort needs to include a continuous outreach to the minority community.

Another area that organizations could zero in on in their board
diversity program is youth. A number of organizations across the
country are placing teens on their boards. The national organization, "Youth On Board" in Watertown, Massachusetts, (*http://
www.youthonboard.org*) provides training in service on governing
boards for young people and training for organizations on how to
place young people on their governing boards. To achieve a repre-

sentative diversity, boards need to design a long-term diversity recruitment plan for their organizations.

5

Governance and Strategic Planning

*Life in a nonprofit organization is no different from the
experience of the average individual American: we all face
a future of rapid transformations—social, political, economic
and technological—as well as one filled with dramatic
uncertainty.... Exceptional nonprofits know that looking
to the future, working to anticipate change and perceiving it
as a challenge and an opportunity will lead to more
positive consequences of these powerful trends for
our communities, our country, and our planet.*
—Edward Steckell, PhD, and Jennifer Lehman

A board of directors' contribution is meant to be strategic, the
joint product of talented people brought together to apply their
knowledge and experience to the major challenges facing the organization. Chait states "strategic plans are badges of legitimacy," but
only if they are implemented and periodically reviewed.[1] Committees, work groups, and task forces need to mirror the institution's
strategic policies. It is difficult "to think of any organization that has
sustained some measure of greatness in the absence of goals, values
and missions that become deeply shared throughout the organiza-

tion."[2] To do the work, trustees and management must determine the important issues and the agenda of the organization. This can't be achieved in a thirty-minute session. Board members need to understand what the CEO and other key senior staff see as the critical issues. They also need to know what each other thinks as well as the perceptions of the organization's constituencies.

Strategic planning is one of a board's most important tasks. Boards need to implement strategic thinking and planning with the management. "Breakthrough strategies, impelled by new ideas, enable organizations to explore new opportunities and capture new markets."[3] A good, workable strategic plan requires commitment on the part of those involved as well as board support.

Experience indicates that to do strategic planning well takes time and attention to details. Usually this entire project takes fourteen to twenty hours and possibly longer. This time span is comprised of two to four hour sessions plus a seven-to-eight hour retreat. To move the process along, the time span between sessions needs to be kept short ... ideally no more than four weeks.

Twenty years ago the focus for organizational strategy was on long-range planning, which focused on a seven-to-fifteen-year span of time. However, this approach was mechanical and deterministic, and its underlying assumption was that the organization's knowledge about the future was sufficiently reliable that it could assume its goals would be attainable. Today the future is fragile, and at best difficult to predict. Next week can be in flux—and maybe even tomorrow.

But what does strategic planning involve? "Strategic planning deals with a new array of factors: the changing external environment, competitive conditions, the strengths and weaknesses of the organization, and opportunities for growth. Strategic planning is an attempt to give organizations antennae to sense the changing environment. It is a management activity designed to help organizations develop greater quality by capitalizing on the strengths they already have."[4]

Strategic planning assumes the future is dynamic and difficult to predict. "Strategic planning is a systematic process through which an organization agrees on—and builds commitment among key stakeholders to—priorities which are essential to its mission and responsive to the operating environment.... The process is strategic because it involves choosing how best to respond to the circumstances of a dynamic and sometimes hostile environment."[5] Thus "strategic decisions are fundamental, directional, and future-oriented."[6]

The board should take responsibility for engaging in strategic planning every three-to-five years. The board is also responsible for evaluating annually the progress being made in achieving the plan's goals and objectives. If necessary, goals and objectives can be altered to fit the current situation. This exercise should be done with staff.

There are eight key steps in the strategic planning process:

- Issue Identification

- Historical Perspective

- SWOT Analysis

- Surveying Stakeholders

- Mission Testing

- Vision Building

- Goal Setting and Objective Building

- Assignment and Cost Analysis

Issue Identification

The number of participants usually is determined by the size of the organization. A small organization may have just the board and staff participate, whereas a large organization may have a strategic planning committee composed of board members, staff, volunteers, and members or individuals the organization serves. The process involves succinctly articulating the issues confronting the organization, asking why they are issues, identifying the consequences of not responding to specific issues, and acknowledging whether each issue is strategic or operational.

Historical Perspective

An individual or small group of individuals should be assigned to write a short history of the organization and distribute it to the committee for review. This history should include the current focus of the organization. When completed, the history represents the organizational baseline, which focuses everyone's attention on where the organization is and how it got there.

SWOT Analysis

A good strategic planning process includes a SWOT analysis. SWOT stands for the Strengths, Weaknesses, Opportunities, and Threats facing the organization This activity examines each of these areas. Besides providing a lot of valuable information about the challenges facing the organization, the SWOT exercise also lends itself to writing a vision statement that expresses where the organization wants to go. Vision is an image of success. Vision is a destination to reach.

Before this exercise begins, the participants need to refocus their minds. Usually all participants think they understand where the organization is in its developmental stage, or in other words, they have a Current View of the Situation (CVS). However, they need to acquire a Better View of the Situation (BVS). Our CVS is based on our collective experiences, which in turn are based on our perceptions which themselves are based on our prior experiences.

But how can we reach beyond the CVS to the benefit of the organization? One way is to observe how other teams work together to create a BVS. Try to get a copy of the July 13, 1999 ABC program, *Nightline*. In particular, view the part of the show, "The Deep Dive," that portrays how a diverse group of people came together to come up with a visionary design for a supermarket cart, a product that everyone usually comes in contact with at least once a week.[7]

The board should take the following steps: Begin the SWOT Analysis by creating a matrix on newsprint. Purchase the kind that has a sticky edge so that it can easily be affixed to a wall for all to see. If the group is large, it might be wise to assign teams of individuals to work on the specific tasks of identifying the strengths, weaknesses, opportunities, and threats within the SWOT Analysis. Give teams at least twenty minutes to meet and generate ideas within their respective category. Everyone will have a chance to comment on what was written down when the small groups report on what they have generated. This process presents a good structure from which to begin visioning exercises along with soliciting input from stakeholders.

Surveying Stakeholders

Based on the analysis, the ideas, issues, and concerns raised ideally will need further assessment and input from the organization's constituencies. This exercise will not only provide input as to what the Strategic Planning Committee has come up with in the SWOT Analysis, it will be an "essential first step toward improved communications.... The reason is obvious. If you don't find out in advance how your target audiences think, feel and react to different issues of concern to you, it will be much harder for you to reach them effectively in language they can understand."[8] One way to gather their input is by using a questionnaire in the form of a survey. Surveys can be conducted by mail, phone, in-person interviews, and the Internet. A good resource for conducting a survey using the Internet is Surveymonkey.com (*http://www.surveymonkey.com*).

Constructing a good survey is very important; however, doing so is not easy. The decision needs to be made as from whom to solicit comments, what questions to ask, how to solicit the information, what information needs to be tested, and how to state the questions so that the questions and their responses do not bias or skew the information being sought. This takes skill. Input should be gathered from the various constituencies or stakeholders regarding what things are working and what are not. Once the information is tabulated and compared to the results of the SWOT exercise, the results can be used in testing the mission statement's relevance.

Mission Testing

The mission statement should be reexamined to see if it needs substantial revision or at least a little tweaking. A mission statement should be brief and direct, running no longer than four to six sentences. If it is longer, return to the basics of what the organization does.

Here are two examples. The first articulates the ideals of the organization, but it is too wordy:

New Literacy Horizons' mission is to teach adult learners, using individual tutors and in-group settings with a trained facilitator, to read, speak, and write English so that they can function in their communities, workplace, and family.

The second example succinctly states the organization's raison d'être:

New Literacy Horizons' (NLH) mission is to assist adult immigrants in learning to read, speak, and write English.

There is no need to explain in the mission statement how NLH accomplishes this, or who else may be involved.

Vision Building

When the information has been collected, it is time for the board to build a vision for the organization. A vision provides direction. A vision anticipates what the organization will be in the future … approximately three to six years from the present. A vision helps the organization focus forward. However, although focused on the future, a vision accepts the potential instability of tomorrow and beyond. It accepts the possibility that certain future events may affect it, but it recognizes the importance of keeping one's eye on the end result.

Begin this exercise with brainstorming what the organization might look like in the future. If the group is too large, it should be split into two. Based on the ideas and perceptions generated from the survey and the SWOT Analysis, brainstorm the direction the organization should take. The objective is to create a "shared vision." "The practice of shared vision involves the skills of unearthing shared 'pictures of the future' that foster genuine commitment and enrollment rather than compliance."[9]

If two groups work at this, bring them together to begin to develop a consensus. The group has reached consensus when most of the group agree on the key points, and those individuals who disagree still agree to support the majority.

Of course, it would be great if a true consensus could be reached where everyone agrees on all the points. However, this usually is a very time-consuming and difficult process. Nonetheless, it is important to persevere and try to achieve it.

The analytical process described should provide the board and staff with an understanding of the current and previous strategies that led the organization to where it is today. It should help assess the effectiveness of the organization's current programs and identify any additional strategic issues or challenges facing it. From here it can raise and answer key questions, and set goals and objectives for the next few years.

Goal Setting and Objective Building

With the mission ratified, goals can now be articulated. They should cover all aspects of the organization's operations, including governance. A goal is a key element in fulfilling the mission of the organization. For each goal, three to six objectives should be created, with an objective being a critical point along the stage to goal fulfillment. It is a step in goal fulfillment where one can measure the progress to fulfilling the goal. Goals are actions that lead to fulfilling the mission:

Objective → Goal → Mission → Vision

Assignments and Cost Assessment

Each specific area with its goal and its objectives ought to identify the projected dates when they will be accomplished. These should be listed beside the goals. The same process should be used for objectives. Equally important is identifying who is responsible for completing each goal or objective. Write the individuals' initials beside the goal and objective. Make sure there is also a place to acknowledge when the goals and objectives are accomplished. To help monitor the progress, create a format that best meets your organization's needs, and share it with staff and board. Alternatively, use the format in the example below, which makes use of a spreadsheet. Notice it lists the area of operation first.

Here is an example for Resource Development also known as fundraising:

Nonprofit Organization Strategic Plan		Date	Individual	Done
Resource Development				
Goal 1: Increase Fundraising by 50% by 2006		6/30/06	DW	
Objective				
1	Create corp. program	12/31/05	AC	
2	Personalize annual appeal	10/30/05	KL and Board	
3	Institute spring tele-thon	5/15/05	KL & AC	
4	Research MA founda-tions & write grants	1/30/06-3/1/06	JQ BF	
Goal 2: Create Related Business Income for Organization		9/30/06	AC	
Objective				
1	Brainstorm business concepts	2/1/06	AC	

2	Do SWOT analysis	3/1/06	Staff and Board
3	Create business plan	4/1/06	Staff
4	Seek technical assistance grant	4/15/06	BF

This represents just one area or segment of the operation of an educational, health, religious, or charitable nonprofit organization.

Most organizations have approximately eight basic areas or sectors that are needed in concert to get it on the pathway to success. They are (1) governance, (2) management, (3) financial management, (4) resource development or fundraising (which in this case includes related business income), (5) human resources, (6) marketing/public relations, (7) program or services, and (8) physical plant.

These areas may be figuratively represented in a wheel, which represents the total organization. Each operational area or department is represented by a sector of the wheel. Consider this as being a bicycle wheel. In a bicycle, the spokes hold the wheel together. Remove spokes, and the wheel most likely will collapse. Similarly, each department of an organization's operations usually is crucial to its long-term success, as each department or sector has a role to play. The various departments of an organization provide it with structure so that it can function and move along toward its vision. The wheel may look like the example below, with the size of the segments depending on how they rank in importance and consume operational time of the organization:

Segments of the Organization's Operation

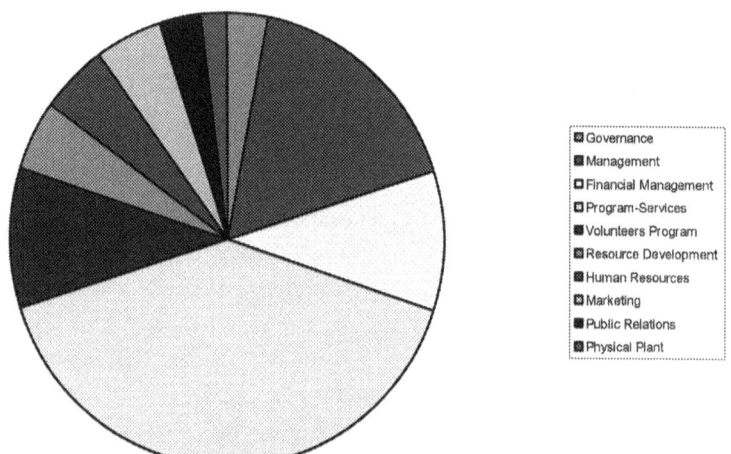

Governance
Management
Financial Management
Program-Services
Volunteers Program
Resource Development
Human Resources
Marketing
Public Relations
Physical Plant

There are numerous workbooks available to help staff and boards do Strategic Planning. An ideal guide and workbook for this process is *Strategic Planning for Nonprofit Organizations* by Michael Allison and Judith Kaye (1976). The book comes with a CD from which one can print out many useful forms.

6

Issue-engaged Boards and Their Evolution

Never doubt that a small group of thoughtful,
committed citizens can change the world, indeed,
it is the only thing that ever has.
—Margaret Mead

Issue-engaged Boards

In chapter 4, it was pointed out that the first part of strategic planning, the issue identification exercise, always stimulates a board's thinking about the key issues confronting the organization. As a prime component to the planning process, the identification of the important issues presents an opportunity to refocus board meetings to spend a sizeable amount of time discussing and resolving these issues. The synergy of the discussions usually leads to identification of other related issues, thus generating substantive and significant discussions. I call this process the *issue-engagement task*. Therefore boards that focus a significant amount of their meetings on discussing substantive issues are *issue-engaged boards*.

Issue-engaged boards set aside a reasonable amount meeting time to discuss pertinent issues confronting the organization. In a board meeting scheduled to last two hours, an hour might be dedicated to discussing one or two key issues (i.e., an issue that has an immediate or future impact on the functioning of the organization.) The issues may focus on funding sources, communication, lack of appropriate vision, organizational growth and its impact on staff, or any other relevant topic.

Board members have the responsibility to raise issues they see as impeding the direction and growth of the organization. Unfortunately, not every board member is willing to point out the issues that are of concern. An individual may be hesitant to raise a question out of fear the issue will not be taken seriously, the flow of the meeting will be interrupted, or other board members will be upset about their areas of responsibility not getting enough attention.

Some individuals would rather not discuss issues that make them uncomfortable. Others are comfortable with the way things are and see no reason to change the format or substance of the meetings—after all, things are going well.

Meetings usually follow an agenda in which the secretary, treasurer, and staff reports are followed by committee reports, which can easily consume two hours, as committee chairs want to report to the board on what their members have been accomplishing. Often the real issues facing the organization never seem to get discussed; and after two hours have gone by, everyone will be tired or focused on their next destination.

Sometimes the work of boards becomes indistinct from the work of staff, which also creates a problem, as "boards are saddled with agenda items that should be left to staff."[1] The agenda gets muddled, and there appears to be no time for issue-focused discussions.

To refocus meetings like this requires at least one confident individual to speak up and begin the discussion, and ideally two. This can happen in a number of ways. Here are two scenarios. First, the CEO or board chair actively seeks a new board member with savvy governance skills. After observing a number of meetings, the new board member perceives the issues and notices they aren't being discussed. The member then waits for the opportunity to have a one-on-one conversation with other board members. After this occurs and others confirm the new board member's observations, the concurring members may be ready to take action to raise the issues that have long been avoided by the entire board.

An alternative opportunity might arise in the strategic planning process. Here the question may be raised as to what key issues are confronting the organization. With the participation of board members, the issues are identified and then brief explanations are given as to why they are issues. For example, let's say that 90 percent of a certain organization's income comes from government funding. A brief explanation is then given as to why this is an issue, and the consequences of not responding to the issue are identified. Finally the issue is identified as being strategic and/or operational.

With one or more issues out on the table, the board, under the leadership of an able chair and key board members, enters into a meaningful dialogue. The word *dialogue* has its origins in ancient Greece. "To the Greeks, *dia-logos* meant a free-flowing of meaning through a group, allowing the group to discover insights not attainable individually."[2] Here the group begins to function as a team with suspension of assumptions and genuine "thinking together."

Richard Chait refers to this dialogue that focuses on key issues as generative thinking, while Peter Senge refers to it as "learningful dialogue." These are conversations "that balance inquiry and advocacy" and at the same time allow individuals to "expose their thinking effectively and make that thinking open to the influence of others."[3] I refer to this concept as issue-engagement or issue-engaged discussions. With issue-engaged discussions, two things need to happen. First there has to be a commitment to get at the truth within issues. Second, board meetings need a new format; otherwise, there will not be enough time for the board meeting.

When discussing issues, it is important to recognize there usually is a range of opinions, resources, and information within a board of directors. Each member brings to discussions a perspective based on the member's experiences. Taken together, the board's collective perspective has the potential to be stronger and more accurate than any individual's. This requires a commitment to dialogue, openness, and complete honesty.

Governing boards that fully understand their responsibilities and are aware of every major action the nonprofit takes hold issue-engaged discussions. At the same time, each member of the board "must act with such care as an ordinary prudent person would employ," and each board member "must act in good faith and in a manner that you reasonably believe is in the best interest of the organization."[4]

The best way to ensure there is enough time for these discussions is to make certain that all committee and staff reports are sent to the board at least a week (or ideally two) before the meeting. It is incumbent upon board members to read the reports and ask the board chair to set aside time for specific questions. Sometimes the board chair may be reluctant to give up the chair's authority in crafting the board meeting agenda, but there is no way around this. To lead, the chair must empower the rest of the board to participate in drafting the agenda. It is the chair who has the responsibility to make sure there is adequate time at every meeting to have discussions about key issues. On the other hand, it is up to the rest of the board to make sure the issues are "on the table" for discussion, even insisting on this if necessary.

Board agendas need to allow adequate time for the issues to be discussed, thereby providing opportunities for the participants to engage in stimulating and creative thinking. It is here the governing board and its CEO "frame problems and make sense out of ambiguous situations—which in turn shapes the organization's strategies, plans and decisions."[5]

The results of issue-based discussions will have a substantial impact on the organization, its board, management team, staff and volunteers. The greatest impact eventually will affect the organization's clientele. Equally important is the fact that issue-engagement stimulates board participation and attracts potential board members with the right skills. Issue-engaged boards stimulate "fire-in-the-belly" attitudes that are a motivating force in board members who have a sense of passion for what the organization is accomplishing.

The chair can encourage issue-based discussions by posing these questions:

What are the key issues confronting the organization? What issues do you think we should discuss at the next board meeting? The board's responses should be listed in the agenda. When the board meets, the issues should be framed by the constructs of:

• Why is it important?

• What are the consequences of not responding to the issue?

• Is the issue strategic or operational?

This is the same format used in the strategic planning process. Its focus is the present and the future. Issues should be framed the same way; as most of the time, they have a historical context. The board members and/or staff who have been with the organization over a period of time can share their valuable historical perspective. While issues should not be bound to the past, it is important for boards to keep in mind that understanding the past empowers them to understand the present and shape the future of their organizations.

One of the keys to the success of this process is collegiality among board members. It is important they view each other as colleagues, as "dialogue can only occur when a group of people see each other as colleagues in mutual quest for deeper insight and clarity."[6] Creating a sense of collegiality is a cornerstone to the process of dialogue. Within a governing board, it requires time for people to get to know each other. It also requires trust.

The reality is that colleagues don't need to agree or share the same viewpoints. One can still be a colleague and have a difference of opinion. It is always easy for collegiality to reign when everyone agrees, but it is more difficult when there is significant disagreement. However, it is important to keep in mind that colleagues are entitled to have differences, even significant ones. Each person should listen to colleagues' points of view, all of which are based on the unique experiences of those individuals.

As colleagues engage in an issue and participate in dialogue, there is great need to focus on exploring the convergent and divergent viewpoints. Focusing on a specific issue requires good listening skills, a willingness to explore key issues, and an affinity for grasping the potential complexity that may lie within. This means listening and weighing alternative viewpoints. This approach in board discussions leads to a thorough understanding of the issue.

Once all aspects of the issue are out on the table, the board chair can move the meeting toward identifying the relative outcomes the board wants to achieve vis-à-vis the specific issue. This may require further discussion. One thing to keep in mind is that this process often will generate new thoughts and perspectives relative to the issue presented, which is an ideal process. The board chair should apply the concept of group consensus as the board tries to resolve the issue. In a group consensus, the majority agrees to the desired resolution, but those who disagree state their disagreement and then agree to support the viewpoint of the majority.

Issue-engagement requires a willingness to play with new ideas. It also requires trust, as the discussion will yield different viewpoints along with their defenses. It is important to understand that "in order to produce trust, individuals must entrust themselves to others."[7] They must recognize their own. vulnerability or their fears of placing themselves in a vulnerable position.

As issue-engaged discussions occur, it may become necessary or at least helpful to have certain tasks carried out by smaller groups, particularly the task of gathering information and seeking options. It is important that such committees and task forces work in service of the board and spend only those resources the board thinks the committee's output is worth. The extent that this can be accomplished will often depend on the size of the board and the stage of development the board and the nonprofit have reached.

But what if no one responds to the board chair's original request for issues that need to be discussed? Instead of proceeding with the notion that there are no pertinent issues to analyze, set aside part of the next board meeting and raise the following questions:

• What should be at the top of the board's agenda next year?

• What are the most attractive, least attractive, or most worrisome aspects of the proposed Strategic Plan?

• What external factors will most affect the organization in the next year?

• What are we overlooking at the organization's peril?

• What is the most valuable step we could take to be a better board?

By asking questions, and then asking more questions as you arrive at different levels of understanding, you sometimes discover issues. Asking the right question helps you understand as much of the entire operation as possible. It leads to what Daniel Boorstin, former head of the Library of Congress, refers to as understanding "what you didn't know you didn't know." This very process lays the groundwork for the board's evolution. However, it should not be confused with micromanaging, which is managing with excessive control or attention to details.

As part of this process, boards need to understand the organizational chart and the responsibilities of staff. They need to be able to follow what is happening financially, both month-to-month and quarter-to-quarter. If there is anything that anyone doesn't understand, it is incumbent on that person to ask questions and on the rest of the board to respect the inquiry and help clarify.

In many of the cases presented in earlier chapters, some or all of the board members were not informed of what was transpiring, even though "a board member has the right to be informed. Perhaps nothing else so hampers effective decisions as the failure on the part of the board members to understand the issues involved."[8] Likewise, the withholding of information or unintentional lack of communication can impede an organization's growth and development.

The Evolutionary Stages of Nonprofit Boards

There are three stages in the development of nonprofit governing boards. The size and status of the organization usually indicates the level of their development. New organizations generally begin through the leadership of an individual or a small group of individuals. If the organization is founded and organized by an individual, it generally operates by following the leader's directions. The governing board is small in size and homogeneous, and it is not task-oriented. The board members act as the staff. A similar start-up nonprofit may be created by a group of individuals. Here too, the board is small and homogeneous, but the members tend to have the time and energy to take on tasks and to feel a sense of ownership. They operate in an informal manner and are hesitant to hire staff, as they are the organization's active volunteers. Eventually they may hire a CEO, but as a member of the staff—a "go for," not as a leader.

The next stage in board development is the transition board. This is a board that has come to the realization that it can't cope with all the tasks before it. It realizes it needs fundraisers, financial managers, committees, new and experienced board members, and a real CEO—one with leadership qualities. This CEO is hired, and in turn, hires staff within the parameters of the budget. This CEO usually provides support to the board in its governance activities.

Here the board may truly assume the role of governance. It creates nominating and board development committees. The latter has the responsibility to guide and sharpen the board's governance skills. In turn, the staff accepts its role in being accountable to the board, and the board accepts its responsibility in helping to fund the organization as well as its role in maintaining organizational integrity. Founding members may or may not be part of the board or staff at this stage. If they are, their influence should be on the wane.

On occasion, boards in this stage have difficulty perpetuating themselves as well as moving along the growth continuum. In this situation, it is a good idea for the CEO to gently nudge the board to fulfill its obligations. The CEO as well as board members ought to become familiar with the variety of resource materials on governance from BoardSource (*http://www.boardsource.org*).

It also is at this stage that the organization begins to grow and become diverse. This board is no longer involved in the day-to-day operations of the organization, but instead holds the CEO accountable for them. It is within this stage that a strong working dynamic develops both among board members and between the board and the CEO.

In the third stage, the board moves from a transitional to an institutional board, which is one that perpetuates itself, fully recognizes its fiduciary and strategic planning responsibilities, and gladly assumes fund-raising and related duties. Its members are leaders in their communities and professions. The institution these board members represent is usually highly regarded in the community.

When a board attains institutional status, the organization generally is successful. This nonprofit now requires a larger, stronger board. It recognizes that it needs to add new people to marshal more financial resources and participate in governance responsibilities. At the same time, the board's importance increases. It understands the need to delegate to stronger independent committees. This board is ready to perpetuate itself. It is issue-engaged.

Institutional boards tend to be very large and diverse. Many of their members have the capacity to give—and to give generously. At all times, institutional boards retain their governance role and their ultimate legal authority. They accept new responsibilities. Recruiting new members is not difficult, as there are always individuals who would like to serve on them. Institutional boards often delegate governance to an executive committee. This type of board brings on members capable of attracting other new members. The officers and nominating committee have influence and outreach.

Institutional boards usually have no more than twenty-five to thirty members with a governing or executive committee of ten to twelve members. (As noted in chapter two, future federal legislation may limit the size of these boards.) Fundraising is a major activity of this board. These boards often have goals, and the staff has objectives to measure their progress in attaining them. They assume that their organizations' professional staff will follow approved plans and operate the organization in a reasonable manner. Boards in the earlier stages of development also have strategic planning, fund-raising, and financial overseeing as their responsibilities. However, it is the institutional board that completely understands the ownership of these three areas and usually does not require prodding from the CEO to assume responsibility for them.

7

A New Work Ethic for Nonprofit Organizations

Every great social movement begins first as an idea in the mind of one person. But no individual can build and preserve an institution alone.
—Cyril O. Houle

Board Development as an Essential Component of Good Governance

"Effective Governance by the board of a nonprofit organization is a rare and unusual act. Only the most uncommon of nonprofit boards functions as it should by harnessing the collective efforts of accomplished individuals to advance the institution's mission and long term welfare."[1]

One of the most important tasks a board can do to counter this accusation and begin to build toward effective governance is to create a Board Development Committee. Nonprofit boards of directors share the responsibility of supervising the operation of their organizations as well as developing and maintaining best practices in their governance activities. The ideal process for ensuring this happens is to establish a board development committee.

Board development is the process of constantly working at effective governance by creating more accountability, generating more measures of success, improving governance skills, and instituting best practices in governance. Every nonprofit organization would benefit from the creation of a Board Development Committee. This committee, with the support of the entire board, assumes the responsibility to help the board enlarge its knowledge of best practices in governance while at the same time sharpening their governance skills. The committee also assists the board in focusing on "what matters most," which includes:

- Helping recruit and interview prospective board members

- Providing orientation for new board members

- Assigning mentors to new board members

- Providing training sessions on the art of governance

- Creating mini-workshops on new issues in governance

- Assisting with board performance and analysis

- Identifying beneficial assessment processes

- Providing board members with the opportunity to access board development materials and internet resources on governance

- Guiding the board in exercising its fiduciary responsibilities

- Instituting a conflict of interest policy for the organization covering board and staff

- Ensuring the board reviews the strategic challenges facing the organization.

- Focusing the board on diversity and community building

- Stimulating cordiality among board members through social activities and an annual retreat.

Finally, the Board Development Committee should be charged with the task of ensuring that a group of talented people, entrusted with the responsibility of governing its organization, will apply their full knowledge, experience, and governance skills to the challenges facing the organization. A board's contribution is strategic when the joint product of its talented members applies their knowledge and experience to the major challenges facing the organization.

What Nonprofit Governance Can Learn from the Corporate World

While there are obvious differences between for-profit corporations and nonprofit ones, many of the principles of good corporate governance set forth in Sarbanes-Oxley are equally applicable to the nonprofit sector. Given the absence of shareholder oversight, and in light of recent abuses involving charitable assets, the requirement to employ financial controls can help ensure the integrity of charities by deterring mismanagement and misconduct while allowing financial problems to be discovered in time to fashion remedies. Charities need to follow stricter rules for fiscal soundness and transparency. With their tax-exempt status, these charities don't have to pay taxes, while at the same time they gain the ability to fundraise from the public.

There are some American corporations with excellent governance principles that ought to be looked at by the nonprofit sector. General Electric is one of these. It has these principles of governance:

- The board has the responsibility to select, evaluate, compensate, and oversee the CEO as well as the succession process.

- The board has the responsibility to provide counsel and oversight on the selection, evaluation, and compensation of senior management.

- The board has the role of reviewing, approving, and monitoring fundamental financial and business strategies and major corporate actions;

- The board has the responsibility to understand the major risks facing the corporation and to approve steps to mitigate those risks.

- The board has the responsibility to ensure structures and processes are in place to protect and advance the company's integrity and reputation—including the accuracy and completeness of its financial statements; the compliance of the organization with legal and ethical requirements; and the quality of its relationship with its employees, customers, suppliers, and other stakeholders.

General Electric also has a process for evaluating board and committee effectiveness. These tasks fall to the Nominating and Corporate Governance Committee. "Every November, an independent expert in corporate governance will contact each director soliciting comments with respect to both the full board and any committee on which the director serves. These comments will relate to the large question of how the board can improve its key functions of overseeing personnel development, financials, other major issues of strategy, risk, integrity, reputation and governance. In particular, for both the board and the relevant committee, the process will solicit ideas from directors about:

a.   improving prioritization issues;

b.   improving quality of written, chart, and oral presentations from management;

c.   improving quality of board or committee discussions on these key matters;

d.   identifying how specific issues in the past year could have been handled better;

e.   identifying specific issues which should be discussed in the future; and

f.   identifying any other matter of importance to board functioning."[2]

The Board and Human Resources

Most nonprofit organizations do not have human resources departments, but boards ought to have a personnel committee. Because boards are responsible for setting policies, they are ultimately responsible for making sure that a personnel policy exists. This policy should be reviewed by the organization's counsel. Overall, the policy ought to make use of "Richard Walton's eight criteria for evaluating the quality of working life in an organization," meaning this document should do the following:

- Ensure there is adequate and fair compensation, including benefits, for all employees

- Insist on safe and healthful working conditions

- Provide opportunities for management to use and develop the human potential that lies within the staff

- Create and make use of future opportunities for continued growth and security

- Integrate the workforce by encouraging supportive work groups marked by reciprocal help, social-emotional support, and affirmation of the uniqueness of the individual

- Establish a framework of basic rights of privacy, free speech, equity, and due process

- Make sure that staff work responsibilities do not outweigh or take up leisure and family time on a regular basis

- Create a personnel manual and make sure all of the above are articulated within it.[3]

The human resource committee needs to focus not only on job descriptions, but on an entire benefit package that includes medical insurance, life insurance, vacation time, disability income, and retirement plans. Employees are often provided benefits according to their status. However, the high cost of benefit packages is impacting organizations, and boards are making the tough decision to pass on the extra costs to the employees, especially in non-executive classes. At the same time, executive compensation with benefits is rising significantly. Examples abound in the corporate sector, and fortunately or unfortunately, in the nonprofit sector as well, depending on the situation.

Here is what is happening in some mid-size nonprofit organizations: An organization that we'll call the Want-To-Look Institution (WTLI) has an approximate operating budget of $2.5 million. All of the employees of this nonprofit, who are in their fourth, fifth, and sixth years of employment, were originally guaranteed payment of their health insurance by the organization. Suddenly the rules change. Now WTLI is faced with a $50,000 operating loss and an increase in health insurance costs of roughly 14 percent. The board along with the CEO sees no choice but to pass this expense on to the employees. The employees are suddenly saddled with a $400 a month expense for health insurance taken from salaries that range between $30,000 and $40,000 a year. At least two employees are major family providers. One can imagine the impact on these employees' family expenses.

At the same time, the CEO who is being paid over $150,000 a year is given a substantial raise of 6% while the organization operates substantially in the red. Because the CEO's spouse is the provider of his family's health insurance, the CEO negotiates with the board to receive the value of the health insurance offered to all employees as additional salary. His salary now has increased to $175,920. In addition, this CEO also has a $10,000-a-year car allowance. As for the rest of the staff, they only received a two percent raise. Was the CEO's increase in compensation based on a superlative annual board evaluation? The board had not performed an annual evaluation of the CEO. In fact, the CEO's new compensation package never was presented to the whole board for its approval. It was only approved by a few board members. What are the values that encompass this work environment? What are the values at work within the process of governance at WTLI? Has the board ever even taken the time to identify their values?

An article in the October 23, 2005, Sunday edition of the *New York Times* points the finger at directors who fail to consider shareholder (and within the nonprofit sector, this means stakeholder) "interests before those of managers." The term *stakeholders* refers to all parties who have a vested interest in an organization. A nonprofit organization's stakeholders include clients, patients, students, customers, corporate members, the general public, finders, employees, consultants, suppliers, regulators, volunteers, trainees, neighbors, researchers, professional societies, trade associations, and board members.

CEOs often negotiate with the board regarding their compensation. Their argument for significant salary and benefits is that a less-than-high compensation package indicates to their employees that the board lacks confidence in the CEO. However, if employees have a lack of confidence in their CEO, it is based on performance, not compensation.

"In view of the pension and health insurance givebacks being forced upon low-level workers, this surge is especially obscene … What is in it for me is the way we live now." The setting of CEO compensation by the board president or the finance committee without discussion and approval by the full board indicates a lack of due diligence on the part of the board.[4]

Because within the corporate and nonprofit sectors, CEO compensation is being scrutinized due to various corporate scandals, here are some recommendations:

• The board or its delegated committee should determine CEO compensation without input from the CEO.

• CEO compensation in the nonprofit sector ought not to exceed 10 percent of an operating budget between $500,000 and $999,999; 7 percent if it is $1,000,000 or more; 5 percent if it is $2,000,000 or more; 4 percent if it is $4,000,000 or more; and 3% if it is $6,000,000 or more.

• The CEO benefit package should not exceed 16% to 22% of a base salary, with a smaller percentage for higher salaries and a higher percentage on lower ones.

• CEO and senior executive benefit packages should not be paid in cash.

• There is a great need for compensation equity among all employees.

• It is important to focus on the compensation needs of all staff, not just senior staff.

Cost of living pay raises significantly impact the senior staff because they are already being well paid; however, they generally have little impact on those who make less than $50,000 annually.

Fortunately, there are some new trends on the horizon, at least in corporate America. Employers are trying to shift health costs, because "rising health insurance premiums are toughest to absorb" for low-wage workers. To offset the trend of rising healthcare costs, companies are adopting salary-based plans. In these plans, "employers pass on more of their rising healthcare costs to well-compensated executives than they pass on to lower-paid workers who can't absorb the dramatic premium increases." This is an emerging strategy that needs to be explored by the nonprofit sector. Well-compensated staff members who don't take health insurance would still have to absorb some of the cost by an internal payroll tax or deduction. "Some top executives say they don't mind paying more under salary-based plans, which appeal to their sense of equity." Other companies just feel it is the right thing to do.[5]

Nonprofit boards need to explore all these existing options. There are solutions—it just takes time and energy to find them. For example, how many nonprofit organizations have looked at flexible benefit plans? These are plans that provide direct benefits to all the staff, usually in the form of allowing employees to use pre-tax dollars to pay for a variety of out of pocket medical expenses such as co-pays for doctor visits and prescriptions. Other benefits besides health insurance include life insurance, dental insurance, disability insurance, disability income, and retirement savings. For medium-to-large nonprofits, the cost of operating these plans can be outsourced at great savings.

It is equally important for board members to make sure the work ethic of their organization is fair, just, and considerate; in fact, it is their fiduciary responsibility to do so.

While the focus of every nonprofit is its programs, true success in each respective program must be built on a "people first" philosophy. This can only come about when board members become aware of the issues facing their staff. "In the physical universe, the very act of observing something changes it."[6] Take note that people are attracted to "and perform their best for leaders who serve them."[7]

Quantum physics teaches us that everything in our world is interrelated and connected to everything else. We each can have an impact on all the people in our immediate universe, in our workplace, and in the world. Boards and their executives can have an impact on the staff and the nonprofit's client base, and they can individually impact the world. Let's reach out to try to meet the needs of the staff of our organizations.

8

The Power of Ethics in Governance

We must be the change we wish to see in the world.
—Mahatma Gandhi

_____

The Role of Ethics in Nonprofit Organizations

What is the role of integrity in our society? Before answering that question, let's define some basic concepts. *Integrity* is the adherence to moral and ethical principles, encompassing honesty. *Ethics* are a system of moral principles. *Morals* are principles or habits with respect to right or wrong conduct. *Virtue* is moral excellence: goodness; righteousness; conformity in life and conduct to moral and ethical principles. Finally, *Values* are ideals or customs that arouse an emotional response.[1]

During the past few years, there has been an onslaught of newspaper articles about corporate and nonprofit malfeasance. Here are some of the headlines of newspaper articles concerning nonprofit organizations that have appeared in the *Boston Globe* and *New York Times*:

"Travel Expenses Prompt Yale to Force Out Institute Chief." "Charity Named in a Home-Selling Tax Suit." "U.S. to Monitor

Big Medical School After New Jersey Fraud Accusations." "Senators Press Red Cross For a Full Accounting." "New Treasurer at Harvard Tied to Inquiry." "Thousands Missing in Revenue Records of Culinary Charity." "DeLay Charity for Children Financed by Corporations." "Report Says Ex-A.I.G. Chief Defrauded Foundation 35 Years Ago." "A Rift Opens at A.C.L.U. Over Issues of Fund-Raising and Leadership." "Report Faults Orchestra Officials on Deal for Rare Instruments." "Boarding School's Rector, Under Fire, Will Step Down." "BU Trustees Retreat on Conflict-of-Interest Goals." "N.H. School Head Fired Amid Concerns." "Groton School Trustees Indicted." "Citing Conflicts, Getty Museum Director Quits." Mostly likely, articles like these have appeared in major newspapers across the United States.

In each of these situations, was everyone involved mindful of their fiduciary responsibilities? What and where were their ethics? What happened to their integrity?

With newspaper articles like these, is it possible to create a climate of integrity within America's nonprofit organizations? What of the multitude of problems that potentially exist in America's smaller and medium-size nonprofits? Malfeasance, poor communication, failure to abide by internal controls, and outright theft combined with lying, manipulation, obfuscation, and even changing the rules seem to creep into the nonprofit world on a daily basis. But much of this can scoot by the eyes and ears of governing boards because they choose not to be informed about how their nonprofit is run.

These boards gloss over the responsibility of assessing the performance of the executive director, the organization, and themselves. They fail to heed the recommendations listed in the management letter written by the organization's auditors. They choose not to create an overarching credo or management philosophy for the organization. Conflicts of interest on the part of the board and the management team are not a concern. Integrity is not paramount in the operation of the organization, or it is given only lip service.

Those who abuse the public trust either lack a sufficient grounding in the ethics of Western civilization to enable them to internalize what they should have learned at an early age, or they never had the opportunity to explore them in a values-clarification setting. For example, the teenager who arrived, his freshman year, at his college campus upright, honest, concerned, and forthright. Faced with a personal crisis thirty years later, he chose what was expedient and in his personal interest regardless of whether the action was right or wrong. When he and other individuals like him are overwhelmed by a crisis, they can't see the importance of wrapping themselves in a blanket of courage and values to get through the crisis, be it personal, professional, or organizational.

Collectively, state and federal governments bestow on us a public trust to maintain and nurture the nonprofit organizations in this country. The responsibility we assume as fiduciaries is a sacred trust. Yet, we are negligent in our responsibility and in our obligation to ask the right questions, and we demonstrate our ineptness in sharing with colleagues what is really on our minds.

Every organization needs to examine itself. For those that set integrity as the prime approach to their operation, keep it up and write about your philosophy and how it supports the organization's successes. Articulate the values under which your organization operates. Make sure the board and the staff pledge to operate with these values. Publicize them. Live by them.

What is the role of truth or honesty in our daily lives? Is it in the process of getting lost? What is the origin of truth? What is its origin in Western thought? And what has this to do with governance anyway? The answer lies in the fact that we have lost contact with the very ethics that are the basis of our upbringing.

The ethical principles upon which we operate in most of the Western world and especially in the United States have their origins in ancient Greece and our Judeo-Christian heritage. "The word 'ethics' has its root in a Greek term meaning 'custom, usage.'"[2]

In ancient Greece, Aristotle clearly outlined the concept of ethics. He said that there were two kinds of virtue, intellectual and moral. "Intellectual virtue in the main owes both its birth and its growth to teaching (for which reason it requires experience and time), while moral virtue comes about as a result of habit, whence also its name *ethike* is one that is formed by a slight variation from the word *ethos* (habit) … Neither by nature, then, nor contrary to nature do the virtues arise in us; rather we are adapted by nature to receive them, and are made perfect by habit.… The virtues we get by first practicing them, as also happened in the arts as well … For the things we have to learn before we can do them, e.g., men become builders by building and lyre players by playing the lyre; so too we become just by doing just acts, temperate by doing temperate acts, brave by doing brave acts."[3] As human beings we must practice ethics from an early age, and like the professional musician, we must practice the craft every day. Our instructors are our parents, our culture and our religion. The "common principle" is to act according "to the right rule."[4] But what happened to the right rule? If it existed in Aristotle's day, it certainly should have become imbedded in our heads and hearts after Moses received the Ten Commandments from God. Let's see how this evolved.

The Israelites entered a covenant relationship with God. This relationship based on faith involved not scattered individuals, but the community as a whole. God chose the community, and the community accepted him and his directives, establishing an "entire moral attitude." The Prophets expanded upon these moral imperatives. Christianity entered into this covenant through the persons of

Jesus and Paul, who as Jews embodied the moral ideals of the prophets.[5]

"The essential task performed by the Hebrew prophets and the Greek philosophers for the ethics in the West was the creation of a basic moral personality. Since their times, at least until the twentieth century, individuals and communities have been able to look back to persons in either or both of these ethical communities to say, 'they established our identity.'"[6]

If this ethical heritage is an intricate part of the Western world, what has happened to our ability to internalize the ethics of this heritage and implement them in our personal and professional lives? Where is our integrity? Given this heritage, the corporate world speaks very little about standards of integrity, although we expect and require "integrity standards of almost every profession. Standards of corporate integrity, much like standards of personal integrity become an issue when people experience distrust."[7]

Up until the past four or five years, the corporate world carried on business as usual with only a few entities operating with a sense of integrity. Johnson and Johnson is an example of one such organization. (Refer to its credo in chapter 3.)

In the nonprofit world, organizations may be focused on their mission, but how many are really operating their organization on a humanistic and 100 percent ethical basis? Where is your organization? Don't look just on the surface of things. Is there teamwork? Is it promoted and rewarded? Or does the CEO quietly or overtly operate with a "me first" attitude?

Because the nonprofit sector is created as a public trust, there is only one road to follow, and that road is built on the ethical and moral principles of our Judeo-Christian heritage. There ought to be zero tolerance for individuals who are ethically and morally weak, even if they have some skill or attribute that would be an asset to the organization. Therefore, our governing boards must be comprised of ethical and moral individuals.

But where do we begin to build this sense of organizational ethics? One place to start is by identifying one's individual values, and then identifying what the group believes the organization's values ought to be.

Values and the Nonprofit Organization

What is our personal value system, and what is our organization's value system? Do these value systems clash? If so, what should we do about it? For example, the way a board handles organizational compensation should be based on the organization's values. Or if a board decides to hire a part-time fund-raiser, how will this action affect the underpaid CEO who works more than the thirty hours for which she is paid? Should the board allow this to happen? Here is a four-step exercise you can do with your board.

A Values Exercise:
What are your organization's values?

- First, have each board member underline eighteen of these values that they feel are important for your organization;

- Second, have them cross out six of the eighteen that are the least important;

- Third, have them circle eight of the remaining underlined ones they feel are the most important. (Try this process by yourself so that you have a feel for how it works):

- Fourth, have someone facilitate the responses.

Values to contemplate

| Kindness | Resourcefulness | Integrity | Loyalty |

Helpful	Honesty	Justice	Gratitude
Optimism	Humility	Teamwork	Visionary
Fairness	Ingenuity	Genuine	Knowledge
Prudence	Promptness	Diligence	Harmony
Valor	Creativity	Compassion	Quality
Stability	Happiness	Courage	Perseverance
Security	Bravery	Mercy	Accountable
Prestige	Passion	Curious	Wisdom
Spiritual	Privacy	Democratic	Expertise
Efficiency	Competence	Achievement	Effective
Excellence	Cooperation	Community	Ethical

The facilitator should have the board members compare their individual results by sharing them with their colleagues. Do this using newsprint, overhead projector, blackboard, or PowerPoint. Have the board members place a star or check mark beside the eight values they selected. The facilitator now should try to get consensus on only eight values by eliminating peripheral ones.

Is everyone in agreement? Is there consensus? If not, can you move toward consensus? By consensus, it is meant there is a majority in agreement, with the minority stating their disagreements but indicating their willingness to accept and support the will of the majority. The facilitator should try to get everyone in the group to move toward consensus.

Values belong in the workplace. They ought to be a part of the philosophy of the organization where they should mesh with its articulated goals. On one level, there is the mission of the organization—the purpose. Then there is the philosophy of how the organization will function, and the guidelines it will use to conduct its business internally and externally. These guidelines should be based on a set of values. The board is responsible for setting the values and guidelines by which it operates. It ought to include input from the staff, and then make its decision binding on the board and staff, meaning that both accept and are committed to it.

Positive institutional values have a direct bearing on the motivation of the worker. They influence the worker's attitudes and affect the whole organization "where the dignity of human endeavors" is recognized rather than exploited. Many changes will need to take place to achieve such a place.[8] Value systems always enhance the well-being of others.

"Nothing short of a people-first philosophy will drive successful enterprises in the near future."[9] Boards and their CEOs will have to examine how they are functioning and what they are really achieving. Herein lies the most difficult part … observing how we interact, play the game, and explore the concepts upon which we made our most recent decisions. A value-focused organization will recognize that values are best evolved in a marketplace of ideas, one that supports a learning environment. The governing board, along with its CEO, ought to be the driving force behind this approach. A value-focused organization also will examine not only the ethics by which it operates, but also whether the means it is employing are delivering the end results it desires. This requires a systematic, scheduled process entailing an assessment of how the organization is functioning.

A people-first philosophy is an ethically bound philosophy. It ought to be clearly and succinctly stated in an organization's credo. If the organization doesn't have a credo, now is the time to articulate one, as it is as important as the organization's mission and vision. An ethical approach to running the organization will have a significant impact on the whole organization: board, staff, clients, donors and all other stakeholders. Make integrity the focal point of your organization's operations. It is the only way to fit into the modern world without the organization losing its soul.

Certainly not all values evolve from Western culture, as cultures and religions such as the Baha'i Faith, Confucianism, Mohammedanism, Shintoism, Hinduism, Zoroastrianism, and Buddhism likewise contribute to human value systems. How these will impact corporations and nonprofit organizations in America is still evolving.

9

The Board and the Process of Assessment

Every reflection, including one on the foundation of human knowledge, invariably takes place in language, which is our distinctive way of being humanly active.
—Humberto R. Maturana, PhD, and Francisco J. Varel, PhD

Organizational Assessment

Organizational assessment is part of the planning process. It is related to strategic planning, but it has a focus of its own. Just as individuals benefit from assessing how they are living their lives and what they are accomplishing, organizations need to be constantly evaluating just what they are doing. Why does your organization exist? What do you and your colleagues and others involved in this organization want to achieve? How are you moving toward these goals, and at what cost (human and monetary)? The self-assessment process is an act of self-discovery.

There are four basic kinds of evaluation tools: Program, Accounting, Staff, and Governance. Each are important, so none should be overlooked. The assessment process requires support of the board and the management team. It also requires participation of stakeholders.

For program evaluation, the Self-Assessment Tool of the Drucker Foundation is excellent. The "Drucker Foundation Self-Assessment Tool" is administered by individuals who have been trained and approved by the Drucker Foundation, which maintains a list of qualified people at their website, *http://www.pfdf.org*. This process strives to assess what the organization is doing, what it is supposed to be doing, and whether it is accomplishing it.

Another approach to explore is the Logic Model. There are a number of sources for this model, which focuses on outcomes and the means to achieve them. An excellent one can be found at the University of Wisconsin's Extension Service, *http://www.uwex.edu/pdande/evaluation/evallogicmodel.html.*

Two options exist for assessing how an organization's accounting process is performing. If the organization has an annual audit, it is important to have the auditor evaluate how the accounting system is working and report the findings and recommendations in a management letter. If the organization is small, it will usually have an accountant review the financial statements at the end of the fiscal year. But in this situation, it is impossible for anyone to fully assess the organization's accounting process. It is up to the board to determine how the accounting is being handled, with this process reflecting on how well it is performing its fiduciary responsibilities. Checklists in Jody Blazek's *Financial Planning for Nonprofit Organizations* are useful for this purpose (see pages 36-39, 95-99, 132–135, 174–183, and 233–243.)

Evaluating staff performance is also important for the organization and for each of the staff members. It is the board's responsibility to insist that evaluations be performed annually, but it is the CEO's responsibility to evaluate the staff, with managers in turn evaluating the individuals who report to them. The board always has the responsibility to evaluate the CEO. A variety of evaluation tools can be found on the Internet. Whatever tool is chosen for the staff ought to be used as well in the evaluation of the CEO.

One of the newest trends in the nonprofit world is to use 360-degree evaluation tools. With this tool, four to eight individuals who work and come in contact with the CEO, within the organizational community, are asked to provide feedback to the board on his or her performance.

The focus of this process is on improving performance. While most of the individuals would be employees of the organization, one or two might be external stakeholders such as a major donor and/or a member of the community in which the organization operates. Community might be defined as a town or city or, if the organization derives its operation from a national entity, a national organization. It is the board's responsibility to initiate, coordinate, and report a summary of the results to the CEO in a timely manner. The names of the individuals participating in the assessment are never revealed to the CEO.

However, boards should not use personnel evaluation tools like the '360-degree' to terminate an employee; rather, they should be used to help an individual grow professionally.

While the 360 degree evaluation appears to be a valuable tool, boards should be aware that some studies have raised doubts as to the effectiveness of this tool. Therefore boards should carefully explore use of this tool before implementing it.

Board Evaluation

The self-assessment process also involves determining how the board is performing its governance job, both individually and collectively. This doesn't require a great deal of effort and can be completed in a number of steps. Excellent resources can be found at *http://www.boardsource.com.*

One step a board can easily implement is to design and complete an extensive board profile, which would include an analysis of skill sets among the board members and of board diversity attributes. These two analyses will point out the strengths and weaknesses of the board and focus attention on the kinds of individuals and skill sets that would enhance it.

This simple assessment tool can be created by making a grid using an Excel spreadsheet. On the top row, enter the name of a board member and the date. Then make a list of the background information and skills that ideally should be represented on the board. For background information, one might have:

Occupation	Heritage (race, cultural and or religious)
Age	Years on Board
Marital Status (including number of children)	

Skill sets might include:

Marketing	Fundraising
Finance	Construction
Education	Legal
Risk Analysis	Management
Public Relations	Research
Facilities Management	Strategic Planning
Real Estate	Governance
Investment Management	Networking
	Assessment and Evaluation

Have the board members rank their skills using a scale of zero to four with:

> 0 = not sufficient knowledge, but willing to learn
> 1 = some knowledge
> 2 = good or average knowledge
> 3 = very good or above average knowledge
> 4 = excellent or very knowledgeable

After soliciting input from everyone, create the same grid, but list every board member in the left column so that the results of each individual's assessment can be entered on a master sheet. When all the results are on one spreadsheet, there should be a subjective but fairly accurate picture of the collective skills of the board. For example, if there are a lot of threes and fours under Public Relations, the organization's board is well represented in this area. If there are a lot of zeros and ones under Fundraising, it is evident the board is weak in this skill. Another way to judge is to note the average score under each category. Look at the example that appears over the next two pages:

Board Skills Assessment

Name	Occupation	Age	Marital Stats	Heritage	Member since -/-/-	Skills Accounting	Assessment & Evaluation	Financial Planning	Fundraising
Jane Doe	manager	38	married	white	1/1/00	3	1	3	3
David Kav	life coach	69	married/1 child	white/Jewish	3/1/03	2	1	0	4
Larry Bachrack	banker	44	married/2 child	white	4/1/05	4	2	4	4
Kelly Diamond	founder	86	married	white	6/1/70	1	2	2	2
Missy Tagalot	secretary	33	married	white	9/1/02	1	0	2	1
John Katz	professor	56	single	white/Jewish	2/1/03	0	4	3	3
Patty Wurst	lawyer	40	married/1 child	black	11/1/03	2	2	3	3
Nick Pelantino	librarian	51	married/3 child	white/Italian	5/1/99	0	2	1	2
Stephanie Lagos	scientist	44	divorced/2 child	white/Greek	4/1/02	2	4	3	3
Maggie White	artisan	29	single	white	1/1/06	0	0	0	1
William Blank	retired	72	widowed	white	9/1/98	1	0	3	3
	contractor								
Total						16	18	24	29
Average						1.45	1.64	2.18	2.64

Rate your skills in these areas. 4 = excellent or very knowledgeable; 3 = very good or above average knoweledge; 2 = good or average knowledge. 1 = fair or some knowledge; 0 = not sufficient knowledge to be of help, but I am willing to learn.

Board Skills Assessment

Name	Access To Funders	Governance	Investment Management	Legal	Management	Marketing &/or P.R.	Networking	Politics	Real Estate	Research	Strategic Planning
Jane Doe	3	3	2	1	4	3	3	0	0	0	3
David Kay	0	4	1	2	4	2	3	0	0	0	4
Larry Bachrack	3	3	4	2	3	3	4	0	4	0	3
Kelly Diamond	1	0	0	0	2	1	1	0	0	0	2
Missy Tagalot	1	0	0	0	2	2	1	0	0	0	1
John Katz	3	3	0	1	2	2	1	0	0	3	3
Patty Wurst	2	0	0	4	3	2	2	0	4	3	3
Nick Pelantino	2	0	0	1	1	1	1	0	0	2	1
Stephanie Lagos	3	0	0	2	2	2	2	0	1	4	3
Maggie White	1	0	0	0	0	2	0	0	0	0	0
William Blank	3	0	2	2	3	2	1	0	3	0	2
	22	13	9	15	26	22	19	0	12	12	25
	2.00	1.18	0.82	1.36	2.36	2.00	1.73	0.00	1.09	1.09	2.27

Rate your skills in these areas. 4 = excellent or very knowledgeable; 3 = very good or above average knowledge; 2 = good
1 = fair or some knowledge; 0 = not sufficient knowledge to be of help, but I am willing to learn.

Any score less than 1.0 indicates a severe weakness in the category. For example, "Investment Management" has a score of .82. The individual results in the column shows that only one board member, "Larry Backrack," perceives himself as having excellent skills in this area. However, it is important that there be at least two or three individuals with skills in this category, especially if the board is managing the endowment.

Now examine the "Fundraising" column. Here the average is 2.64. When we look at the individual scores in this column, we find five individuals who rate themselves as very good, two who rate themselves as excellent, and two who rate themselves as good. The remaining two indicate they have some fundraising knowledge. This indicates the board either is a fundraising board or certainly has the potential to be one.

Notice that this board currently is made up of eleven members. However, the bylaws of this organization permit fifteen members. This board needs to actively search for potential board members to fill the four vacancies. Three good resources are your local United Way Board Bank, Boardnet USA (*http://www.boardnetusa.org*), and networking.

As skill sets of individual board members are examined to see which ones are missing and needed, every board should closely examine itself and determine which skills are important to the process of governing with an ethos of excellence within its articulated set of organizational values. The entire board ought to make the commitment to help develop strategies on how and where to seek the kinds of people who will strengthen the board and enable the organization to grow and fulfill its mission.

Another board assessment tool follows. Its criteria are Governance, Fiduciary, Strategic, and Issue-engagement. These categories indicate how well a governing board is doing its job. There is no arbitrary score to achieve, but every governing board should strive to be as close to 100% of each category as possible.

This assessment can be done individually or both by individual board members and the board as a whole. If done in the latter format, make sure the chair of the board places this on the agenda and sets aside adequate time to do the exercise. Why do it as a whole board? Because there may be areas with which you may not be familiar, but other board members might. If you do the evaluation by yourself and then with the whole board, you may learn things about the operation about which you weren't aware, which is important. Any area that doesn't get a single check is one that certainly needs board and CEO attention.

The Strategic Assessment of Board Performance

Check each item that your board and its organization have achieved.

Governance

The board drafts the CEO's and the CFO's job descriptions.   [ ]

The board meets periodically without the CEO.   [ ]

The board annually reviews the CEO's performance.   [ ]

The board clearly articulates its values.   [ ]

Board decisions may be legally made by telephone and Internet.   [ ]

Board members usually serve on only one committee, and no more than two.   [ ]

Board members are familiar with the Articles of Incorporation.   [ ]

Board members have read and understood the organization's bylaws.   [ ]

New board members are assigned mentors.   [ ]

Mentors understand their role in guiding new board members.   [ ]

New board members are given welcome packets that include: [ ]

Articles of Incorporation

Bylaws

Schedule of board meetings

List of committees and their functions

Minutes of past meetings

Most recent audited statement or financials

Most recent strategic plan

Brief history of the organization

Recent newsletters

List of board members with addresses, etc.

Other information.

There is an active board development committee.   [ ]

An assessment of each board member's skills is done every other   [ ]
year.

An assessment of the board's performance is done once a year.   [ ]

The board is committed to diversity throughout the organization.   [ ]

The board makes an effort to recruit minorities, if applicable.   [ ]

The board takes the initiative in perpetuating itself.   [ ]

Board members feel their participation strengthens the board and the   [ ]
organization.

The board has a process for removing members who are either not   [ ]
productive or not attending meetings.

There is order and process to board meetings.   [ ]

Board members receive committee reports at least a week before   [ ]
board meetings.

Board members truly identify with the mission.   [ ]

The board makes effective use of technology.   [ ]

The board is aware of any vacancies on the board.   [ ]

The board is aware of how the organization is perceived in the com-   [ ]
munities it serves.

The makeup of the board reflects in some way the community it   [ ]
serves.

Tough questions are asked at board meetings. [ ]

There is an informal social program for the board. [ ]

The board and staff understand the concept of social entrepreneurship. [ ]

The board and the CEO have an entrepreneurial mindset. [ ]

The organization created partnerships. [ ]

All board committees are functional and functioning. [ ]

There are term limits for board members. [ ]

There is a process for orienting new board members. [ ]

The board established and maintains a code of ethics for the organization. [ ]

Fiduciary

The board periodically reviews financial controls. [ ]

The board annually reviews the CEO's and senior executives' salaries and benefits. [ ]

The board approves personnel manuals in conjunction with counsel.   [ ]

The board reviews bylaws every few years.   [ ]

The board approves all legal documents including State forms and   [ ]
Federal forms 990 and 990-pf.

The board reviews and approves annual audits.   [ ]

The board approves all contracts.   [ ]

There is directors' and officers' liability insurance.   [ ]

The board maintains a complaint and "whistle-blower" policy.   [ ]

The board as a whole understands financial reports.   [ ]

The board has a written conflict of interest policy.   [ ]

The board annually declares conflicts of interest.   [ ]

The budget has a line item for Board Development.   [ ]

The budget has a line item for professional development that is available to all staff.   [ ]

The board ensures there is strong budgetary planning and implementation.   [ ]

The board understands the sources of income for the organization.   [ ]

If there is no audit committee, then the board or finance committee assumes responsibility for the completeness of the audit.   [ ]

The board chair signs the 990 and other government reporting forms along with the CEO.   [ ]

The board has established a records retention policy.   [ ]

The board treats all organizational data with absolute integrity.   [ ]

The organization is financially stable.   [ ]

The board created an endowment program.   [ ]

Board members are aware of pending state and federal legislation regarding the nonprofit sector.   [ ]

Board members are familiar with the Sarbanes-Oxley Law.   [ ]

Board members participate in fundraising activities.   [ ]

The board is trained in soliciting donations.   [ ]

Fundraising goals are set annually.   [ ]

The board has an active recruitment policy.   [ ]

The board ensures there are adequate resources.   [ ]

The board is interested in equitable remuneration and benefits for all staff.   [ ]

Strategic

The board initiates and participates in strategic planning.   [ ]

The planning process includes a SWOT analysis (see chapter 4).   [ ]

Input is solicited from stakeholders.   [ ]

The mission statement is reformatted as needed.   [ ]

There is a vision statement, written within the past three-to-five years.   [ ]

Goals, objectives, completion dates, person(s) responsible for action, and potential costs are included in the strategic plan. [ ]

The board ensures the strategic planning process is completed in twelve months or less. [ ]

The strategic plan is reviewed annually, and if necessary, revised. [ ]

Issue-engagement

Board meetings allot time to discuss key issues. [ ]

Board members are not afraid to say what is on their minds. [ ]

The board has articulated the outcomes it desires for the organization. [ ]

The board is satisfied with the means (as articulated by the CEO) to accomplish the goals or outcomes. [ ]

The board understands the roles and responsibilities of key staff. [ ]

The board actively communicates with the staff. [ ]

The board has a good working relationship with the CEO. [ ]

In this process of assessing performance, candor, forthrightness, and commitment are needed. Looking at one's performance can be a little threatening. Trust is a crucial ingredient in the process. "In order to produce trust, individuals must entrust themselves to others; they make themselves vulnerable. Before they are willing to take such action, they must examine their fears about what others may do to them, or their fears about designing their own vulnerability."[1]

As boards take action to improve how they function, it is important to realize that "organizations are designed and managed to make management less difficult but human beings act in ways that make management more difficult."[2] Make the commitment to improve the governance side of the operation and the management side will follow. Part of this commitment needs to include taking action toward creating a learning environment.

10

The Board's Role in Creating a Learning Environment

*"The success of a whole community depends on
The success of the individual members, while the success of individual
members depends on the success of the community as a whole."*
—Fritjof Capra

"Change starts with awareness."[1] We usually don't explore the dynamics within ourselves. We also aren't used to looking at our environment. We enter into situations with a variety of experiences that will enable us to leverage them, but it is often difficult to stand outside the box to get another perspective. Yet, we need to do just that.

Too often our perceptions are based on our immediate and long-term experiences. If those experiences are limited in scope because they are solely influenced by the organizations we serve, we limit the tools at our disposal for solving our problems. On the other hand, if we have a broad series of experiences from different settings plus ongoing training in proven techniques acquired in a learning experience, we begin to see new ways to arrive at solutions.

Learning environments are crucial to the development of organizations. "It is individuals acting as agents of organizations who produce the behavior that leads to learning."[2] It is incumbent on boards to make sure the climate exists to create a learning environment, which is one "that is continually expanding its capacity to create its future."[3]

It is the board's responsibility to make sure there are funds for board development and professional development. Board and professional development opportunities lie in local, regional, and national conferences. In addition, the board can make use of consultants, executive coaches, and facilitators for in-house workshops on a specific topic or issue. If board and professional development is important, it needs to be represented as a line item in the budget. Professional development should be available for all the staff, not just the senior administrators.

Likewise, the board should question when there is no line item for professional development. If there is, board members should ask the CEO what is going to be accomplished with the amount being requested and who is going to benefit from it. A learning organization ought to benefit all of the staff. Every experienced CEO knows there is always an opportunity for staff to learn new skills and to get out and meet old and new professional colleagues. While individual learning does not guarantee organizational learning, "without it, no organizational learning occurs."[4]

The structure needs to be set in place for this to happen, as "structure influences behavior."[5] The payoff for positive outcomes abounds.

A learning organization is part individual learning, the sharing of that learning with the team, and team learning. Team learning is a discipline that begins with "dialogue," which is the capacity of members of a team to suspend assumptions and enter a genuine "thinking together" mode. As noted in chapter six, *dialogue* comes from the Greek word *dia-logos*, a conversation or discussion between two or more people in which an idea or concept is expanded upon and one or more participants think through a topic, learn something, gain insight, and/or expand their vision of a topic. In his book, *The Fifth Discipline*, Peter Senge defines discipline as a developmental path for acquiring certain skills or competencies.

Skills are acquired through practice, whether it is playing the piano, driving a car, flying an airplane, or using a computer program. Some of us may have certain intrinsic skills that enable us to master the task more quickly than others, but anyone can master the skills given enough practice and perseverance. We all need to work at improving our competencies, programs, team functioning, and organizations. We also need to be lifelong learners.

Governing boards need to implement this kind of thinking into their board meetings, which tend to be a large bottle full of committee reports with little discussion of the key issues hanging over the future of the organization. It is exceedingly important that a substantial amount of time be set aside for boards to have "'learningful' conversations that balance inquiry and advocacy, where people expose their own thinking effectively and make that thinking open to the influence of others."[6] Management teams also should be having these conversations rather than those "on the fly," which are conversations that take place in the course of sticking one's head in another's office, passing in the hall, or chatting at the coffee machine/water cooler.

Creation of a learning environment lays the groundwork for making wise policy decisions and stepping into the leadership role. Board Development is a crucial part of a nonprofit's "learning environment." 'The Board Development Committee ought to bring something of value to present to the board at every meeting. This presentation should be first on the agenda with the goal of enlightening and focusing everyone on improving how they perform their role as a board member and providing insight to nonprofit governance and management.

Here are some recommendations that will strengthen every board member's governance skills:

1. Join BoardSource, the National Association of Nonprofit Boards, at *http://www.boardsource.org;*

2. Subscribe to the Board Café, at *http://www.boardcafe.org;*

3. Attend a conference with a focus on governance;

4. Read the following books:

    a. *Financial Planning for Nonprofit Organizations* by Jody Blazek

    b. *Governance as Leadership* by Richard P. Chait et al

    c. *On Board Leadership* by John Carver

    d. *Governing Boards* by Cyril Q. Houle

    e. *Primal Leadership* by Daniel Gorman et al

    f. *The Fifth Dimension Fieldbook* by Peter Senge et al

11

Boards as Policy Makers and Leaders

Institutions and movements succeed over the long term
Not because of their cultures, or core manufacturing
Competencies or their use of modern management tools,
But because they continually generate leadership at all levels.
—Noel M. Tichy

Governing boards need to assume responsibility for setting the policies affecting their organizations. Often boards impede their organization's operation by focusing on the day-to-day operations. In the early stage of development, this may be impossible to avoid. Board members may actually be doing the work in running the organization, or the board has hired their one and only CEO/staff who can't possibly do all the work.

However, it is when the organization moves out of stage I of the nonprofit's development into stage II that the board assumes fully the role of policy maker and the staff assumes the role of implementer. It is here the board should take on its role in leadership. If boards focus on their role as the leadership of their organization, they will begin to conceptualize their understanding of governance.

Boards should set aside significant time to enter into dialogues with the CEO and their colleagues about their respective roles in assuming leadership. Learning organizations can't exist in a vacuum of leadership as it requires a commitment on the part of the board and the key players to build a learning organization. Leadership is not about taking the initiative to do a needed task. Leadership is about empowering others to get the tasks done and the goals and objectives accomplished.

The traditional view of leaders is that they are key people who make key decisions and energize the staff. This view is based on the assumption that people are powerless, void of personal vision, and unable to master the forces of change. This view also believes that only a few great leaders can only remedy these deficits.

The new view of leadership in learning organizations is that "leaders are designers, stewards, and teachers. They are responsible for *building organizations* where people continually expand their capabilities to understand complexity, clarify vision, and improve shared mental models—that is, they are responsible for learning."[1] It is fruitless to be a leader in an organization that is poorly designed. "The design work of leaders encompasses designing the organization's policies, strategies and 'systems.'"[2] This is the governing board's role.

Boards need to function not only within the realm of logic, but to be creative and expansive in their thinking. The tension between reality and possibility will play itself out. Fully participating boards are good at this. Boards are the ultimate policy makers responsible for spearheading strategic planning, assuming responsibility for fundraising, and supervising the design of organizational systems.

There is much confusion about the concept of leadership. When it is being exercised, it can be felt throughout an organization. Warren Bennis, author of *Why Leaders Can't Lead* and a noted authority on leadership, points out that leadership instills "pace and energy to the work and empowers the work force. Empowerment is the collective effect of leadership. In organizations with effective leaders, empowerment is most effective in four themes:

- *People feel significant.* Everyone feels that he or she makes a difference to the organization. Where they are empowered, people feel that what they do has meaning and significance.

- *Learning and competency matter.* Leaders value learning and mastery, and so do people who work with leaders. Leaders make it clear that there is no failure, only mistakes that give us feedback and tell us what to do.

- *People are part of the community.* Where there is leadership, there is a team, a family, a unity. Even people who do not especially like each other feel a sense of community.

- *Work is exciting.* Where there are leaders, work is stimulating, challenging, fascinating and fun. An essential element in organizational leadership is pulling together rather than pushing people toward a goal. A 'pull' style of influence attracts and energizes people to enroll in an exciting vision of the future. It motivates through identification, rather than through rewards and punishments. Leaders articulate and embody the ideals toward which the organization strives."[3]

The leadership of a nonprofit organization needs to assume the role of organizational designers. Organizational design is a process that is not readily visible because it takes place behind the scene. It encompasses "an organization's policies, strategies, and 'systems.'"[4] Leadership's first design task concerns first developing a mission, then values and vision. It involves generating the governing ideas, values, and purpose of the organization. It is a strategic task.

The leaders of nonprofit boards must help people/staff understand the seismic forces that shape change. They must focus on seeking out the truth and operating with integrity. In this aspect of their leadership role, they must foster "learning, for everyone."[5] Part of this process involves asking good questions and discovering new answers to old ones. Lance Secretan tells the story of Albert Einstein and a student. "During a university course taught by Albert Einstein, a student pointed out to the great teacher that the questions were the same as the previous semester. Einstein kindly but firmly replied, 'That may be, but the *answers* are different this time.'"[6]

To focus on the issues key to the mission and vision of an organization, the CEO and the board need to manage their time carefully. This is not easy. Boards don't often understand why their CEO can't get everything done at once, while CEOs are often confounded with the problem of managing their time, both professional and personal. The truth of the matter is that board members also have the same problem.

There are four kinds of issues and tasks that come before us every day: the *important*, the *important and urgent*, the *unimportant*, and the *unimportant and urgent*. The board and the CEO need to immediately clear from their agendas the *unimportant* and the *unimportant and urgent* to focus on the *important and urgent* and the *important*. If they have too many issues that fall into the *important and urgent* category, they haven't been spending enough time focused on the *important*. Important issues usually only become *important and urgent* when they have been avoided or not enough time has been allocated to work on them.

Boards ought to be a source of organizational leadership, which is framed by its ability to understand the past, steer the course using the rules of fiduciary engagement, guide the organization through strategic planning, and commit to guiding the organization to becoming issue-engaged. It is from issue-engagement that policy making evolves. The board and its CEO need to focus on these responsibilities, but the CEO must take responsibility for implementing policies, informing the board of any violations by the organization, and implementing programs with a focus on outcomes.

By policy, we mean a definite course of action adopted for the sake of expediency or an action or procedure conforming to or considered with reference to prudence or expediency.[7]

Leadership and policy making are intertwined. "Board members' collective philosophy ... should be central to board policy." It should encompass their collective values. Policies must evolve from the collective dialogue of the whole board.[8]

While there are times that a CEO may recommend policies to the board, it is the responsibility of the board to discuss, examine, and test their validity against organizational values. It is the board's role and responsibility to decree them—not anyone else. The CEO and staff must understand this.

"Not only should the board decide for itself what its policy provisions will be, it should also decide what to have policies *about* and what level of prescriptive or proscriptive detail the policies will go into. It is critical to the integrity of board leadership that the board and the board alone control these documents"[9] The board's wisdom and the institutional values must be reflected in the policies. "When policymaking is properly construed, the board is its policies."[10] Thus values, policy making, and leadership go hand in hand.

12

The Board, Its CEO, and Shared Visions

*—to leave what we have and move out, not without fear,
but without succumbing to that fear. It is a call to redefine
what is possible, to see a vision of a new world and to be willing
to undertake, step-by-step, what is necessary in concrete terms
to achieve that vision.*
—Joseph Jarworski

Boards need to be aware that executives tend "to be blind to their own impact on others." They often "see their relationships with their peers and subordinates in a much rosier light" than do their respective peers, subordinates, and board.[1] At the same time, people generally trust leaders. An organization without a leader is often "more disturbing than continuing acquiescence to mediocre or impulsive executives."[2]

The power inherent in the position of CEO can impede these individuals from protecting themselves from their own excesses. "The pressure of decisions requires some defense against being overwhelmed by information and the complexity of problems. Executives, therefore, often insulate themselves against reality with staffs whose loyalty is primarily to them".[3]

Board members and staff sometimes see executive leadership crumble when individual board members set expectations and make demands of the executive. When it is just one board member, it is difficult. When it is three or four board members, each making different demands on the CEO that clearly should come from the board as a whole, the CEO often becomes very stressed.

Individual members of the board sometimes assume or act as though they are representing the entire board when that authority has not been bestowed on them. In this situation, it is important for the CEO, the board chairperson, and each board member to realize that individual board members can speak only for themselves, not for the board as a whole. Only the CEO works for the board as a whole.

When it comes to giving advice, individual board members can do so to the CEO, but the board as a whole can never take on that role. Its role is to govern. The board should recognize that this is of the utmost importance, as it is the basis upon which the board can make a commitment to the CEO to provide open channels of communication, to make opportunities for nurturing, and to provide an evaluation process that stimulates opportunities for learning as well as personal and professional growth.

"The normal day-to-day relationship between the board and the executive is that of a responsible partnership. Neither of them can mark out any one institutional activity as its central concern, nor can it permit itself to be denied authority over any such activity. Even if the board relieves the executive of responsibility for some function, he still has the obligation to consider it to be part of the whole program and to warn the board when he believes the function is not being adequately performed."[4]

Board feedback on an ongoing basis is important. Opportunities for this abound, but the CEO needs to make sure to communicate with each board member. Board members who live within the organization's region ought to find time to meet with the CEO, one on one, at least once a year, and ideally twice. In fact, it would be best if the CEO initiated the contact, arranging to meet at a convenient time and location. Meetings with board officers at least twice a year are equally important if not more so. The CEO must budget the time to do this and take the initiative in making the contact with the objective being to build communication channels.

Inherent in being the CEO is the role of leadership and the power that the position bestows on the individual. "Power is the potential people have to affect other people's behavior."[5] When it is exercised, it may wreak havoc among the board and the staff, with the end result being a dysfunctional relationship that loses sight of the organization's mission and vision. When there is dysfunction, it is most important to recognize it and try to pinpoint where it is embedded.

While there are tools that can be used for bringing about change, too often current dynamics and relationships are not discussed in depth, and the opportunity to bring about this change within the leadership is missed. The board sees the only answer is to dismiss the CEO. However, this is not the only response. Most boards understand their responsibility to evaluate the CEO, but fail to comprehend their responsibility in setting the values and philosophy of the organization. Such action lays the groundwork for the organizational dynamics in which everyone will operate. The right dynamics help set the tone for creating a shared vision.

Shared Vision and the CEO

The goal is to achieve a successful coalition of the board and the CEO as the leadership team. The best coalition serves the interests of the board, the organization's CEO, and the organization. To this end, the board and the CEO ought to share an organizational vision, which is different from having a personal vision of the organization. A shared vision is not an abstraction, but something shared by the board and the CEO. "When people truly share a vision they are connected, bound together by a common aspiration. Personal visions derive their power from an individual's deep caring for the vision. Shared visions derive their power from common caring.... One of the reasons people seek to build shared visions is their desire to be connected to an important undertaking."[6]

Shared visions tap into an organization's sense of purpose, articulating specific goals, but they must be generated by many individuals and reflected in the organization's purpose. Such visions have the power to engage aspiration and commitment. The board, the CEO, and the senior staff need to be involved in designing the processes by which individuals at every level of the organization have an opportunity to share their heartfelt observations of what the organization is about.

This is where the board and the CEO show their leadership and work as a team. They set the tone, spirit, and attitude for the rest of the staff, empowering everyone in the process. Shared visions are important for the organization as they provide the energy and focus for learning. This happens when the people involved are engaged in building shared meaning, which is a collective sense of knowing what is important and why. It is at this point when everyone has had the opportunity to consider what is important to them that everything begins to come together. As the strands of shared meaning join, they in turn bind the organization together.

Good, responsible governance is crucial to nonprofit development. We ought to be aware that "human beings manifest two kinds of theories of action, one that they espouse and the second that they actually use."[7] This reflects back to the individual's personality and personal vision. When the CEO and the board are truly committed to a shared vision, it reflects back to their personal vision. One cannot have a learning organization without a shared vision. The CEO and the board are the leadership team, with each retaining the potential power to affect the other's behavior. However, this relationship does not alter their individual responsibilities and roles.

13

Reinventing Governance in Nonprofit Organizations

At present, people create barriers between each other
by their fragmentary thought. Each one operates separately.
When these barriers are dissolved, then there arises one mind,
Where they are all one unit, but each person also retains
his or her individual awareness. That one mind will still exist
even when they separate, and when they come together,
it will be as if they hadn't separated.
—Dr. David Bohm

When organizations find themselves in trouble, neither their boards nor their senior executives readily perceive the evidence. Instead they assume an aura of *momentary autism*, a new phrase that refers to the misinterpretation of what the social situation is all about. In essence, they haven't a clue as to what is really happening and don't perceive any evidence of organizational dysfunction.

Board members often have little understanding of the evolution of their organization, the current climate in which it exists, the needs of the client base, the board's fiduciary responsibilities, or the importance of strategic planning, much less what it means to be engaged in discussions that focus on the important issues affecting the organization. Above all, the board fails to assess the performance of its organization, its staff, its CEO, and itself.

Despite this, everyone recognizes that nonprofit organizations today are functioning in a rapidly changing world. The evidence of problems may be all around them, but it goes unheeded. It's not that everyone is oblivious to the mounting data, but that no one has the necessary perspective. To correct this situation, our boards need to be future focused—and the sooner the better. Governing boards can turn their situation into one concentrating on outcomes: effective governance, policy formation, and effective means to implement the policies.

Whatever the situation, the tools outlined in this book are a route to the solution. To get there, boards need to stop and assess where they are and recognize their responsibilities:

- organizational sense of place—know the context in which your organization is evolving;

- fiduciary—recognize the responsibility the government has bestowed on you as a board member and fulfill it;

- strategic—be future focused and plan the organization's vision accordingly;

- issue-engaged—participate in *learningful* and meaningful discussions for the sake of the organization's mission.

Nonprofit organizations are important phenomena in the evolution of our country. They get their impetus to function from the people who create them and from the power given to the governing board by state and federal governments.

Boards ought to be responsible for perpetuating themselves. There are two ways to accomplish this. First, ideally the bylaws should limit the number of terms an individual can serve on the board. Board elections should be staggered, with half the board being elected on even number years and the other half on odd. Second, the board should make sure there is a proactive nominating committee. Unfortunately, there are often times when this does not happen unless the CEO takes the initiative, usually in the form of identifying and meeting potential board members. However, if the nominating committee is merged into the board development committee, this problem may be solved, depending on the level of proactiveness of the committee.

Boards and their nominating and/or board development committees need to continually be on the lookout for prospective board members. They should be expanding each board member's understanding of their role and responsibilities as well as how to be more effective. They also should generate a spirit that "attracts board members, makes them want to work with one another, and gives them a sense of pride and satisfaction in the program and the board itself."[1]

Looking Ahead

In summary, "a strong board is one of the most important ingredients of a successful non-profit. It is up to the board itself to develop the board and ensure its continuity."[2] Governing boards ought to avail themselves of the publications of BoardSource. Besides its annual conference in Washington, DC, each November, BoardSource sponsors workshops and publishes a series of excellent pamphlets and materials, all related to the issues of good governance. The first pamphlet in this series, "Ten Basic Responsibilities of Nonprofit Boards", is excellent. Every new board member ought to be presented with a copy in a 'new board member's welcome packet'.

"In the coming decades, it will no longer be enough to update your mission, develop new programs, or even improve your solving skills. Nonprofit success now depends on your organization's ability to respond to real change with new thinking, new structures, and new linkages to resources."[3]

This requires a fundamental shift of the mind on the part of staff and board members. "If you always think what you always thought, you will always get what you always got."[4] It encompasses adaptive learning and "generative learning that enhances our ability to create." It is built upon our ability to master the key organizational skills and to work on our own self-mastery.[5] "Organizations do not perform the actions that produce the learning. It is individuals acting as agents of the organizations who produce the behavior that leads to learning."[6] The board of directors, along with key staff, have the power to bring about this important new focus. The rest will follow.

One individual out of ten or even a dozen board members is not enough to bring about change in the governance of an organization unless the individual has the ability to persuade others that change is necessary. The key here is to change the mindset of the entire board, or at least the majority of the members.

In his book, *Seven Habits of Highly Effective People*, Steven Covey tells the story of an arborist trying to trim a tree. The man worked all day on a small tree. A man who passed him in the late morning stopped to talk with him late in the afternoon. When he asked the arborist why he was working so hard at trimming the tree, the arborist replied, "I have to do it right." The man retorted, "Why don't you sharpen your saw?" The arborist's response: "I just don't have the time."

This is a good time to sharpen our saws so that we become more proficient in the management, governance, and development of our nonprofit organizations. The board development committee described earlier can foster this focus. If the board is finding it difficult to begin the process, it might be helpful to seek assistance from a professional outside the organization. A consultant or an executive coach who has expertise with nonprofit organizations can assist the board and the CEO in taking a new course of action. Many organizations know what a consultant is, but many have never heard of the concept of a coach. Yet, a professional coach with extensive experience in management and governance of nonprofits may be worth exploring. For more information about coaching and how to find a coach with in-depth experience in the nonprofit world, contact the International Coach Federation at *http://www.coachfederation.org.*

14

Coda

With 1.4 million nonprofit organizations already in the United States and the number growing, it is clear they are a moving force in American society. They intersect our daily lives when we visit our local hospital, arrange for a local charity to pick up our discarded clothes, open our mail, answer calls from our college, or turn on our radio or television.

Each of these organizations has roots that go back further than its own history, and further than we realize, to the English parliament, the early colonies, and the westward movement across this great country. This early American spirit is embedded in our nonprofits. It is what all board members need to bring to the table as they oversee the operation of their organization.

While this book was written for board members, it doesn't make a difference whether you are a board member, CEO, senior executive, or a volunteer of a nonprofit: you are performing an important task. When it comes to nonprofits, there always appears to be more on the plate than can be handled. This book may not lighten the apparent load, but it lays out what is important in governance and the process that needs to take place. This is both your and your colleagues' responsibility. If after reading this book, you determine you can't bring about the necessary change, you are correct—you can't do it alone. However, you can be a catalyst for change by speaking up and talking with your colleagues about the issues presented here.

The goal of this book is to make clear to you what must be done to improve the role of governance in your organization as well as the other nonprofits in America's communities.

There is no doubt this book makes a lot of recommendations, and the task may seem daunting. However, nonprofit organizations always do a waltz with the future: two steps forward, one step back. The important thing is to persevere.

Acquire an organizational sense of place; understand your organization's past and its evolution to where it is today. Map it out on a time line. Next, focus on the board's fiduciary responsibilities. The fiduciary role is the basis of the existence of what I call the social contract between government and the nonprofit entity. The government has bestowed on the nonprofit the right to legally exist and at the same time function as a tax-exempt organization. Then, stir things up by getting the board to initiate strategic planning. Make sure it gets carried through to completion and not left hanging incomplete in mid-air. Finally engage the board, challenge its members' thinking, and bring up issues for discussion that will stimulate them, issues that need to be resolved. It certainly will be rewarding for everyone involved.

About the Author

Arnold Clickstein has undergraduate and graduate degrees from the University of Minnesota and Northeastern University, respectively. He also completed post-graduate study at Boston University. He has thirty-plus years experience as a CEO and teacher in the nonprofit sector with educational and cultural institutions and organizations within regional, national, and international arenas. His experience includes serving on a national management team, as well as the governing boards of local and regional organizations.

Arnold is a member of the International Coach Federation, Organizational Development Network, and Boston Facilitators Roundtable. He is an executive coach, in private practice, who works primarily with CEOs, senior executives, and governing boards of nonprofit organizations. His goal is to help find solutions to the issues impeding the success of key executive staff, their governing boards, and their organizations. Since 2000, he has been in private practice in Winchester, Massachusetts where he lives with his wife and youngest child. On occasion, he leads a seminar on governance for Cambridge College's Institute for Lifelong Learning and Community Building. He has taught at Lesley College (now Lesley University) and lectured at Antioch New England University and Gaigukai University in Japan.

Arnold's clients tend to come from the kinds of organizations that are linked to his personal interests, which are arts and culture, education, and social services, as well as the environment and the outdoors. He believes in the importance of the nonprofit sector and its role in American life. Arnold lives what he teaches.

Visit his Web site at *http://www.strategicwise.com.*

Appendix A

Other Types of Nonprofits

In looking at the nonprofit world in the United States, we need to recognize the broad range of organizations to which Congress through the IRS has granted nonprofit status. Besides charitable, educational, and religious organizations, the following organizations have tax-exempt status:

- corporations organized under an act of Congress

- title-holding companies

- social welfare organizations and civic leagues

- agricultural and horticultural organizations

- boards of trade

- chambers of commerce

- real estate boards

- benevolent life insurance associations

- mutual cooperative telephone companies

- mutual irrigation companies

- mutual insurance companies

- employee-funded pension trusts

- war veteran organizations

- legal services organizations and corporations

- black lung trusts

- veterans' associations formed before 1880

- title holding companies for pensions

- religious and apostolic organizations

- cooperative hospital service organizations

- cooperative service organizations of operating educational organizations

- child-care organizations

- farmers' cooperatives

- nonexempt charitable trusts.

- professional football teams such as the Green Bay Packers and professional football leagues

Certain corporations organized and operated exclusively for:

- scientific purposes

- public safety testing purposes

- literary purposes

- artistic purposes

- health care and public health

- fostering of national or international amateur sports competition

- prevention of cruelty to children or animals

- local associations of employees (membership organizations) whose

- earnings are devoted exclusively to charitable, educational or

- recreational purposes

- labor unions

- business leagues

- local teachers' retirement fund associations

- local benevolent life insurance associations

- cemetery companies owned and operated exclusively for the benefit of their members

- corporations charted solely for the disposal of bodies by burial or cremation

- credit unions without capital stock organized for mutual purposes and without profit

- legal services corporations

- variety of trusts providing a variety of services

- corporations or trusts organized exclusively for the purposes of acquiring and holding real property for the benefit of a qualified pension, profit sharing or stock bonus plan

All of these range in designation from Section 501(c)(1), 501(c)(2) of the IRS Code and continue through to 501(c)(25) and 501(d)–501(k).

Appendix B

Internet Resources for Statistics about Nonprofits

American Association of Fundraising Council
http://www.givingusa.org/about_aafc/index.cfm?pg=charts.cfm

Bureau of Labor Statistics
http://www.bls.gov./newsrelease/volun.nro.htm

Foundation Center
http://www.foundationcenter.org/findfunders/statistics/gm_agg.html

GuideStar
http://www.guidestar.org

Independent Sector
http://www.independentsector.org/PDFs/Inbrief.pdf

John Hopkins University's Center for Civil Society Studies
http://www.jhu.edu/~ccss

National Center for Charitable Statistics
http://www.nccsdataweb.urban.org

National Council of Nonprofit Associations
http://www.ncna.org/index.cfm?fuseaction+page.view-Page&pageID=668&ID=1

The Boston Indicators Project
http://www.tbf/indicators2004/culturallife/overview.asp#trends

Notes

Introduction

1. Wolverton

2. Strom, Stephanie, *New York Times*, September 14, 2004

3. Houle, 6

Chapter 1
The Evolution of Nonprofit Organizations in America

1. National Center for Charitable Statistics, http://
    nccsdataweb.urban.org

2. Ibid

3. Bureau of Labor Statistics, http://www.bls.gov/newsrelease/
    volun.nro.htm

4. Ibid

5. National Council of Nonprofit Associations,
    http:ncna.org/index?cfm?fuseaction=page.viewPage&page
    ID=668&nodeID=1

6. Johns Hopkins University, http://www.jhu.edu/~css

7. Kierkegaard, Vol. I, 450

8. *Encyclopedia Britannica*

9. *Robert's*, 30

10. United States Senate, http://www.senate.gov/artandhistory/no_hissing.htm

11. *Robert's*, 33

12. *Ibid*

13. Supreme Judicial Court of Massachusetts, http://www.massreports.com/about/cushing.htm

14. *Encyclopedia Britannica*

15. The Headquarters, U.S. Army Corps of Engineers, http://www.hq.usace.army.mil/history/coe2.htm

16. *Robert's*, xxxv-xxxvi

17. http://www.hq.usace.army.mil/history/coe2.htm

18. *Robert's*, xxxvi-xxxviii

19. Ibid., xxxix

20. http://www.hq.usace.army.mil/history/coe2.htm

21. de Tocqueville, Volume II, 114

22. Gaul, 8

23. Rusk, 10–13

24. Ibid, 15

Chapter 2
The Role of Government in the Oversight of Nonprofit Organizations

1. Carver, 4

2. Ibid., 4–5

3. Ibid., 79

4. Ibid., 17

5. American Red Cross, http://www.redcross.org

6. Ibid.

7. Ibid.

8. Department of Homeland Security, http://www.dhs.gov/dhspublic

9. Reitman, 43

10. Ibid., 45

11. Ibid., 49

12. Ibid., 76

13. Ibid. 32

14. *New York Times*, May 21, 1991

15. Heller, July 1, 1996

16. FDA Enforcement Report, January, 1, 1993

17. FDA News, April 11, 2003

18. Reitman, 298

19. Government Accounting Office, http://www.gao.gov, September 10, 2002

20. The Raw Story, http://www.rawstory.com, September 13, 2005

21. Seelye, Katherine Q. with Diana R. Henriques, October 27, 2001

22. FDA News, December 13, 2001

23. Ibid., April 11, 2003

24. Ibid

25. http://www.redcross.org

26. Wilke, John R., *The Wall Street Journal*, April 27, 2006

27. U.S. Food and Drug Administration, September 8, 2006

28. Strom, Stephanie, *New York Times*, February 28, 2006

29. Strom, Stephanie, *New York Times*, December 14, 2005

30. Wilke, *Wall Street Journal*, April 27, 2006

31. Adam Nossiter, *New York Times*, March 3, 2006

32. Ibid

33. http://www.redcross.org

34. *Boston Globe*, Editorial, August 31, 2006

35. Strom, Stephanie, *New York Times*, December 18, 2004, A15

36. Moskin, Julia, *New York Times*, September 22, 2004, D1

37. Shenon, Philip & Carl Hulse, *New York Times*, Sept. 29, 2005

38. Rudoren, Jodi, *New York Times*, April 8, 2006

39. Rudoren, Jodi, *New York Times*, April 28, 2006

40. Wakin, Daniel J., *New York Times*, December 18, 2004, 17, 21

41. Ibid

42. Ibid

43. Saltzman, Jonathan, *Boston Globe*, June 8, 2004, B1

44. Ibid

45. Saltzman, Jonathan, *Boston Globe*, April 23, 2005, B1, 5

46. Strom, Stephanie, *New York Times*, May 28, 2005, A7

47. Senator Charles Grassley's e-newsletter, June 22, 2004

48. Discussion draft released by Senate Finance Committee, 1

49. Ibid., 3-4

50. Ibid.

51. Ibid., 13

52. Ibid.

53. Ibid., 14

54. Testimony before the Senate Finance Committee, June 2004

55. Blazek, 33

Chapter 3
A Board Member's Guide to Its Fiduciary Responsibilities

1.   *Random House College Dictionary*

2.   Carver, 165

3.   *Robert's "In Brief"*

4.   Goleman, 163

5.   Carver, 16-22

6.   Ibid., 23

7.   Chait, 159-160

8.   NFP Perspectives, Fall 2002

9.   *Essentials of Accounting*, 5

10. Blaze, 36-39

11. NFP, Spring 2004

12. Corporate Board, May-June 2003,10–14

13. Ibid., 13

14. Ibid

15. *NFP*, Summer 2004

16. Houle, 145

17. Chait, 34

18. Hechinger and Bobowick, 5

Chapter 4
A Fiduciary Addendum: The Board's Role in Fund-raising and Diversity

1. Rusk, 6–7

2. Ibid., 8–9

3. Ibid

4. George, 9

5. Ibid., 1

6. Ibid., 12

7. Carver, 80

8. Ebanks, 10

9. Plummer, 35–39

10. Brown, Center for Nonprofit Leadership and Management

11. DiConsiglio, 4–5

12. Carver, 81

13. Ibid

14. Ebanks, 10

Chapter 5
Other Responsibilities of Governance: Strategic Planning

1.   Chait, 61

2.   Senge, 9

3.   Chait, 62

4.   Cyert, vii, in George Keller's *Academic Strategy*

5.   Allison & Kaye, 1

6.   Ibid., 3

7.   ABC News, # N990713-010

8.   Lindermann, 1

9.   Senge, 9

Chapter 6
Issue-engaged Boards and Their Evolution

1.   Carver, 162

2.   Senge, 10

3.   Ibid., 9

4.   Reilly, 1

5.   Chait, BoardSource, 9

6.   Senge, 245

7.   Argyris, 70 Houle 55

Chapter 7
A New Work Ethic for Nonprofit Organizations

1.   Taylor, 4

2.   http://www.ge.com

3.   Schuster, 4

4.   Morgensen, 1, 4

5.   Blanton, 1, 8

6.   Dibble, 33

7.   Ibid., 55

Chapter 8
The Power of Ethics in the Governance and Management of Non-profit Organizations

1.   *Random House College Dictionary*

2.   Ashby, 25

3.   Aristotle, 181–183

4.   Ibid

5.   Ashby, 90–91

6.   Ibid, 136

7.   Harshberger, 12

8.   Schuster, 291

9.   Dibble, 12

Chapter 9
The Board and the Process of Assessment

1.   Argyris, 70

2.   Ibid., 93

Chapter 10
The Board's Role in Creating a Learning Environment

1.   Dibble, 29

2.   Argyris, 67

3.   Senge, 14

4.   Ibid., 139

5.   Ibid., 374

6.   Ibid., 9

Chapter 11
Boards as Policy Makers and Leaders

1.   Senge, 340

2.   Ibid., 342

3.   Bennis, 23

4.   Senge, 342

5. Ibid., 356

6. Secretan, 8

7. *Random House College Dictionary*

8. Carver, 161

9. Ibid., 161–162

10. Ibid., 163

Chapter 12
The Board, Its CEO, and Shared Visions

1. Argyris, 287

2. Zaleznik, 5

3. Ibid., 6

4. Houle, 86

5. Zaleznik, 44

6. Senge, 206

7. Argyris, 324

Chapter 13
Reinventing Governance in Nonprofit Organizations

1. Houle, 120

2. Gill Foundation

3. Green, 1

4. Haman

5. Senge, 14

6. Argyris, 67

Bibliography

Allison, Michael and Jude Kaye. *Strategic Planning for Nonprofit Organizations.* New York: Wiley, 1976.

American Red Cross, http://redcross.org

Anthony, Robert N. and Leslie K. Pearlman. *Essentials of Accounting,* 7th ed., Saddle River, NJ:Prentice Hall, 1999.

Anderson, Heller, "Chronicle." *New York Times*, February 6, 1991.

Argyris, Chris. *On Organizational Learning.* Malden, MA: Blackwell Publishing, 2002.

Ashby, Warren. *A Comprehensive History of Western Ethics.* Amherst, NY: Prometheus Books, 2005.

Atkinson, Brooks, *The Complete Essays and Writings of Ralph Waldo Emerson*, New York: Random House, 1950.

"The Deep Dive." *American Broadcasting Companies, Inc.*, New York, 1999.

Bennis, Warren, *Why Leaders Can't Lead.* San Francisco: Jossey-Bass, 1989.

Blanton, Kimberly. "Employers shifting health costs." *Boston Globe*, November 25, 2004 business: 1, 8.

Blazek, Jody. *Financial Planning for Nonprofit Organizations*. New York: Wiley, 1996.

Brown, William A. "Center for Nonprofit Leadership and Management." *Arizona State University*, Tempe, Arizona, December 14, 2005.

Bureau of Labor Statistics, http://www.bls.gov.

Capra, Fritjof, *The Web of Life*, New York: Anchor Books, (Random House), 1996.

Carver, John. *On Board Leadership*. San Francisco: Jossey-Bass, 2002.

Carver, John and Mariam Mayhew Carver. *Reinventing Your Board*. San Francisco: Jossey-Bass, 1997.

Chait, Richard P. "The Problem with Governance." *BoardSource, 4,* no. 4 (June/July 2004): 7.

Chait, Richard P., William P. Ryan, and Barbara E. Taylor. *Governance as Leadership*. New York: Wiley, 2005.

"Charity Oversight and Reform, A Discussion Draft." *Senate Finance Committee*. The United States Senate, http://www.finance.senate.gov, 1

Chira, Susan. "After The Flood." *New York Times*, October 20, 1993.

Covey, Steven. *Seven Habits of Highly Effective People*. New York: Merrill, 1994.

de Tocqueville, Alexis. *Democracy in America*. New York: Vintage (Random House), 1945.

Department of Homeland Security, http://www.dhs.gov.

DiConsiglio, John. "Keeping Up With Sarbanes-Oxley." *Board-Source* 12, no. 6 (September 2003): 6–7.

DiConsiglio, John, "The Diversity Dilemma." *Board Member* 12, no. 7 (October/November 2003).

Ebanks, Jacqueline M. "Building Board Diversity." *BoardSource* 12, no. 1 (January 2003).

"Editorial". *Boston Globe*, August 31, 2006.

Encyclopedia Britannica 2003 (software version).

Eliot, T.S., *The Complete Poems and Plays*, New York: Harcourt, Brace and Company, (Harcourt), 1958.

Fairfield, Roy P., *The Federalist Papers*, Baltimore: John Hopkins University Press, (rights now owned by Oxford University Press), 1981

FDA Enforcement Report (January 1, 1993), http://www.fda.gov.

FDA News (December 13, 2001; April 11, 2003), http://www.fda.gov.

Frantz, Douglas. "Blood Bank Politics." *New York Times*, May 30, 1996.

"Governance." *General Electric.* http://www.ge.com.

Gaul, Gilbert M. and Neil A. Borowski. *Free Ride: The Tax-exempt Economy*. Kansas City, MO: Andrews and McMeel, 1993.

George, Worth. *Fearless Fundraising for Nonprofit Boards*. Washington, DC: BoardSource, 2003.

Goleman, Daniel, Richard Boyatzis, and Annie McKee. *Primal Leadership: Realizing the Power of Emotional Intelligence*. Cambridge, MA: Harvard Business School Press, 2002.

Gill Foundation. http://www.gillfoundation.org.

Grassley, Senator Charles. *E-newsletter* (June 22, 2004), http://www.grassley.senate.gov.

Government Accounting Office, Washington, D.C., September 10, 2002, http://gao.gov.

Green, Florence. "10 Things Nonprofits Must Do in the 21st Century." *CAN ALERT*, California Association of Nonprofits, Nov./Dec. 1999: January/February 2000.

Hadas, Moses, *The Basic Works of Cicero*, New York: The Modern Library, (Random House), 1951.

Haman, Gerald. *KnowBrainer*. Chicago: SolutionPeople, 2004.

Harshbarger, Scott and Robert Stringer. "Creating a Climate of Corporate Integrity," *The Corporate Board*, May/June 2003.

Hechinger, Deborah S. and Maria J. Bobowick. "Reclaiming the Board." *BoardSource* 13, (2004):5

Heller, Linda. "The Red Cross: A Question of Competence," *The Nation*, July 1, 1996.

Hong, Howard V. and Edna H. Hong, trans. *Soren Kierkegaard's Journals and Papers.* Bloomington: Indiana University Press, 1967.

Johns Hopkins University Center for Civil Society Studies, http://www.johnshopkins.edu

Houle, Cyrus. *Governing Boards.* San Francisco: Jossey-Bass, 1989.

Ingram, Richard T., *Ten Basic Responsibilities of Nonprofit Boards.* Washington, DC: BoardSource, 2002.

Jarworski, Joseph, *Synchronicity*, San Francisco: Berrett-Koehler Publishers, 1998.

Kaplan, Justin, *The Pocket Aristotle.* New York: Pocket Books, (rights currently owned by Oxford University Press)1958.

Keller, George. *Academic Strategy.* Baltimore: John Hopkins University Press, 1987.

Lindermann, Walter K., PhD. *Attitude and Opinion Research.* Washington, D.C.:CASE, 1983.

Mathiasen III, Karl. *Board Passages: Three Stages in a Nonprofit Board's Life Cycle.* Washington, D.C.: National Center for Nonprofit Boards (now know as BoardSource), 1999.

Maturana, Ph.D., Humberto R. and Francisco J. Varel, Ph.D., *The Tree of Knowledge*, Boston: Shambhala, 1998.

Morgensen, Gretchen. "How to Slow Runaway Executive Pay." *New York Times*, October 23, 2005:1, 4.

Moskin, Julia. "Beard Scandal Scorches Chef Awards." *New York Times*, September 22, 2004, D1

"A Bold Step Toward Safer Blood." New York Times, Editorial. May 21, 1991.

"E-Newsletter" *Nonprofit Quarterly,* Boston, August 2004, Issue 36

National Center for Charitable Statistics, http://nccsdataweb. urban.org.

National Council of Nonprofit Associations, National Council of Nonprofit Associations, http://ncna.org.

Nichol, Lee, *The Essential David Bohm*, London: Routledge, 2003.

The Nonprofit Quarterly, http://nonprofitquarterly.org/section/ 70.html

NFPerspectives. *Grant Thornton.* (Fall 2002): 3.

NFPerspectives. *Grant Thornton.* Vol. 15, no. 1 (Spring 2004)

NFPerspectives. *Grant Thornton.* Vol. 15, no. 2 (Summer 2004):1.

Nossiter, Adam. "F.B.I. to Investigate Red Cross Over Accusations of Wrongdoing." *New York Times*, March 31, 2006.

Plummer, Deborah L. "Race Talk in the Workplace." *OD Practitioner* 36, no. 2 (2004): 35.

Random House Collegiate Dictionary, rev. ed. New York: Random House, 1988.

Reilly, Tom. "An Act to Promote the Financial Integrity of Public Charities." Summary of Draft 1.0 Boston, http://ago.state,ma.us/charity/charitieslegissum.pdf

Reilly, Tom, "*The Attorney General's Guide For Board Members of Charitable Organizations*", Commonwealth of Massachusetts, Boston, January 2004.

Reitman, Judith. *Bad Blood Crisis in the American Red Cross.* New York: Pinnacle Books,1996.

Robert, Henry M. III, W. J. Evans, D. H. Honemann, and T.J. Balch. *Robert's Rules of Order Newly Revised.* Cambridge, MA: Perseus, 2000.

Robert, Henry M. III, William J. Evans, Daniel H. Honemann, and Thomas J. Balch, *Robert's Rules of Order Newly Revised In Brief.* Cambridge, MA: De Capo, 2004.

Rudoren, Jodi. "Special Projects by Congressman Draw Complaints." *New York Times*, April 8, 2006.

Rudoren, Jodi. "F.B.I. Set to Present Subpoenas to Lawmaker's Nonprofits." *New York Times*, April 28, 2006.

Rusk, Dean. *The Role of Philanthropy in American Life.* Claremont, CA: Claremont University College, 1961.

Ryan, William P. "Governance as Leadership." *BoardSource* 13, no. 4 (June/July 2004):9.

Saltzman, Jonathan and Heather Allen. "Groton School Trustees Indicted." *Boston Globe*, June 8, 2004.

Saltzman, Jonathan, "Groton Trustees Said to OK Guilty Plea." *Boston Globe*, April 23, 2005.

Schuster, Frederick E. *Human Resource Management*. Reston, VA: Reston Publishing, 1985.

Secretan, Lance. *Inspire! What Great Leaders Do*. New York: Wiley, 2004.

Seelye, Katherine Q. "Saying that the Board Left Her No Other Choice." *New York Times*, October 27, 2001.

Senge, Peter M. *The Fifth Discipline*. New York: Currency Doubleday, 1990.

Senge, Peter M., Art Kleiner, Charlotte Roberts, Richard B. Ross, and Bryan Smith, *The Fifth Discipline Fieldbook*. New York: Currency-Doubleday, 1994.

Shenon, Philip & Carl Hulse. "The DeLay Inquiry: The Overview; Delay is Indicted in Texas Case and Forfeits G.O.P. House Post," *New York Times*, September 29, 2005

Steckel, Ph.D., Richard and Jennifer Lehman, *In Search of America's Best Nonprofits,* San Francisco: Jossey-Bass, 1997.

Stern, Gary J. The Drucker Foundation Self-Assessment Tool. New York: Drucker Foundation and San Francisco: Jossey-Bass 1999.

Strom, Stephanie, "Public Confidence in Charities Stays Flat." *New York Times*, September 13, 2004.

Strom, Stephanie. "A.C.L.U.'s Search for Data on Donors Stirs Privacy Concerns." *New York Times*, December 18, 2004, A15.

Strom, Stephanie. "Boarding School's Rector, Under Fire, Will Step Down." *New York Times*, May 28, 2005, A7.

Strom, Stephanie. "President of Red Cross Resigns; Board Woes, Not Katrina Cited." *New York Times*, December 14, 2005.

Strom, Stephanie. "Senator Urges Red Cross to Overhaul Its Board." *New York Times*, February 28, 2006.

Strom, Stephanie. "Red Cross Quietly Settles Case of a $120,000 Theft." *New York Times*, April 28, 2006.

Supreme Judicial Court of Massachusetts, http://www.massreports.com

Taylor, Barbara E., R. P. Chait, and Thomas Holland. "The New Work of the Nonprofit Board." *Harvard Business Review* (Sept.-Oct. 1996).

Tessier, Oliver. "Put Me In, Coach." *BoardSource* 2, no. 7 (July/ Aug. 2002).

The Raw Story, http://www.rawstory.com. September 13, 2005

Tichy, Noel M., *The Leadership Engine*, New York: Harper Business, (HarperCollins) 1997.

United States Senate, http://www.senate.gov

U.S. Food and Drug Administration. *FDA News*, (December 13, 2001, April 11, 2003), http://www.fda.gov.

U.S. General Accounting Office, http://www.gao.gov.

Van Bergen, Jennifer. "Investigation Finds Red Cross Agreed to Withhold Orleans Aid,

Operated in Tandem with Homeland Security." *The Raw Story,* (September 13, 2005), http://therawstory.com

Wakin, Daniel J. "Report Faults Orchestra Officials on Deal for Rare Instruments." *New York Times,* (December 18, 2004) 17, 21.

Wilke, John R. "Red Cross Receives New Scrutiny." *Wall Street Journal*, April 27, 2006.

Wolverton, Brad. "Many Americans Are Still Skeptical of Charities." *The Chronicle of Philanthropy*, (September 13, 2004), http://www.philanthropy.com.

Zaleznik, Abraham and Manfred F. R. Vries de Kets. *Power and the Corporate Mind,* Chicago: Bonus Books, 1985.

Recommended Conferences and Websites

Annual conferences are worthwhile attending. Some are appropriate for all nonprofits. Others have a specialty focus like education, museums or historical societies. Explore the websites of these organizations:

ACTA: American Council of Trustees-Alumni
American Association of Museums
Association for State and Local History
Association of Fundraising Professionals
Council for the Advancement and Support of Education
National Association of College and University Business Officers
National Association of Independent Schools
National Association of Nonprofit Boards (BoardSource)
The Alliance for Nonprofit Management
Third Sector New England

Even though the organizations might not be focused in your organization's mission, they all are good resources for board development, financial management and fundraising:

www.aam-us.org
www.aaslh.org
www.afpnet.org
www.boardcafe.org
www.boardnet.org

www.boardsource.org
www.bridgestar.org
www.case.org
www.gillfoundation.org
www.guidestar.org
www.nacubo.org
www.nais.org
www.umwb.org
www.youthonboard.org

Index

Arnold Clickstein has undergraduate and graduate degrees from the University of Minnesota and Northeastern University, respectively, in addition to post-graduate study at Boston University. He has more than thirty years experience as a CEO and teacher in the nonprofit sector.

978-0-595-41714-8
0-595-41714-0